The Penguin Book of Japanese Verse

P9-CJG-394

שי''ח ....35.- N.I.S.
2, Yavetz St., Jerusalem
Tel. 6248237

After reading Greats and Chinese at Oxford, Geoffrey Bownas studied with Professor Shigeki Kaizuka at Kyōto University from 1952 to 1954. He set up the Department of Japanese Studies in Oxford University in 1954 and then became the University of Sheffield's first Professor of Japanese Studies. He established the Centre for Japanese Studies in 1965, pioneering the combination of the study of Japanese with the social sciences. On his retirement in 1980 he was made Emeritus Professor.

He has written and broadcast on Japan since the early 1960s. His books include *New Writing in Japan* (1972), which he edited with Mishima Yukio, *Business in Japan* (1974 and 1980), written with Paul Norbury, and *Japan and the New Europe* (1991), a special report for the Economist Intelligence Unit. His broadcasts include programmes on Japanese culture for the Third Programme, *The Asian Phoenix*, a series for Radio 3 in 1972, and the series *Inside Japan* for BBC TV in 1980.

He has visited Japan regularly since the 1950s.

After leaving Oxford in 1955 Anthony Thwaite went to Tokyo University where he taught English Literature until 1957. He has frequently revisited Japan, holding a Japan Foundation Fellowship for 1985–6, and going on various lecture tours.

He has also taught in other universities in Britain and abroad, was literary editor of the *Listener* and then the *New Statesman*, and co-editor of *Encounter* for the period 1973–85. He has published twelve books of poems, most recently *Selected Poems 1956–96* (1997), and was awarded an OBE for services to poetry in 1990. He is married to the biographer Ann Thwaite and lives in south Norfolk.

UNESCO COLLECTION OF REPRESENTATIVE WORKS
JAPANESE SERIES

This book has been accepted in the Japanese Literature Translations series
of the United Nations Educational, Scientific and Cultural Organization
(UNESCO).

The Penguin Book of Japanese Verse

Translated and with introductions by
Geoffrey Bownas *and* Anthony Thwaite

PENGUIN BOOKS

PENGUIN BOOKS

Published by the Penguin Group
Penguin Books Ltd, 27 Wrights Lane, London w8 5tz, England
Penguin Putnam Inc., 375 Hudson Street, New York, New York 10014, USA
Penguin Books Australia Ltd, Ringwood, Victoria, Australia
Penguin Books Canada Ltd, 10 Alcorn Avenue, Toronto, Ontario, Canada m4v 3b2
Penguin Books (NZ) Ltd, Private Bag 102902, NSMC, Auckland, New Zealand

Penguin Books Ltd, Registered Offices: Harmondsworth, Middlesex, England

First published 1964
Published in Penguin Books 1964, 1998
10 9 8 7 6 5 4 3 2 1

Translation and introduction copyright © Geoffrey Bownas and Anthony Thwaite, 1964, 1998
All rights reserved

The moral right of the translators has been asserted

Every attempt has been made to contact copyright-holders.
Any omissions will be made good in subsequent editions.

Set in Monotype Garamond and Linotype Syntax
Typeset by Rowland Phototypesetting Ltd, Bury St Edmunds, Suffolk
Printed in England by Clays Ltd, St Ives plc

Except in the United States of America, this book is sold subject
to the condition that it shall not, by way of trade or otherwise, be lent,
re-sold, hired out, or otherwise circulated without the publisher's
prior consent in any form of binding or cover other than that in
which it is published and without a similar condition including this
condition being imposed on the subsequent purchaser

Contents

POEMS FROM NOTO. *Noto is on the northern coast of central Japan. It is suggested that the second poem may be a children's song, accompanying or giving the time for a game.*

KAKINOMOTO HITOMARO *(late seventh, early eighth centuries). Hardly anything is known of the life of the greatest of the poets in* Manyōshū.

YOSAMI *(late seventh, early eighth centuries). Wife of Hitomaro.*

HITOMARO KASHŪ, Hitomaro Collection, *probably compiled by Hitomaro and including poems by other poets.*

PRINCE HOZUMI *(d. 715). Fifth son of Emperor Temmu, acting Prime Minister from 705 until his death.*

TAJIHI *(mid Nara period).*

ŌTOMO TABITO *(665–731). After leading an expeditionary force in Kyūshū, was appointed Governor-General of Dazaifu in 728, returning to become Councillor of State in the capital. Most of his extant poems come from his last years. Also wrote in Chinese and was deeply influenced by Taoist thought.*

YAMANOUE OKURA *(660?–733). Went to China on the staff of the ambassador in 701 and was deeply influenced by Chinese thought. Served with Ōtomo Tabito at Dazaifu in 729–30, then made Governor of Chikuzen. Wrote also in Chinese and compiled* Ruijū Karin *(Forest of Classified Poems), which is no longer extant.*

KASA KANAMURA *(early eighth century). Court poet of the early part of the Nara period. His datable poems span the years 715–33. The* Kasa Kanamura Collection, *compiled by him, includes poems by other authors.*

YAMABE AKAHITO *(d. 736?). Early-middle Nara period. The last datable poem is from 736. His poems are representative of the early Nara period and he is cited alongside Hitomaro in the Preface to* Kokinshū.

TAKAHASHI MUSHIMARO *(early eighth century). Served in the provincial government of Hitachi in the reign of Empress Genshō (715–23), and probably had a hand in the compilation of* Hitachi Fudoki, *a kind of gazetteer, which came out at the time. His lyrical long poems, often written round legendary episodes, give him his distinctive position among* Manyō *poets.*

KAMO TARUHITO *(early eighth century).*

LADY ŌTOMO OF SAKANOUE *(eighth century). Younger sister of Tabito, aunt of Yakamochi. Her elder daughter married Yakamochi. Sakanoue, the home of this branch of the clan, is the present Ikoma district. Lady Ōtomo followed in her brother Tabito's retinue on his appointment to Dazaifu in 728 and returned to the capital in 730. Her latest known poem is dated 750.*

ŌTOMO YAKAMOCHI *(?716–85). Eldest son of Tabito. The man most intimately connected with the compilation of* Manyōshū, *as well as being represented by the greatest number of poems – over five hundred – in the collection. His last poem, dated 759, is the latest-dated poem in the collection. His official career was chequered, and included the Governorship of Etchū, at the age of 29, appointment as Vice-Minister for War in the 750s, then relegation to the Governorship of Inari in 758. He was posthumously deprived of his rank and the clan broke up as a result of a crime committed by one of its members.*

Heian Period (794–1185)

ONO TAKAMURA *(802–52). Not very successful as an official Japanese representative in China. Scholar of Chinese and composed in Chinese as well as Japanese.*

ARIWARA NARIHIRA *(825–80). The model of* Ise Monogatari, The Tales of Ise, *in which his poems are given prose contexts and headnotes, so that they become more intelligible in their setting. Tsurayuki said that his poetry 'had too much spirit and too few words, like a fading flower, its colour gone but its scent remaining'.*

MIBU TADAMINE *(early tenth century). One of the compilers of* Kokinshū, *and one of the 'Thirty-six Poetic Geniuses'. Author of a critical work,* The Ten Styles of Japanese Poetry.

MINAMOTO MUNEYUKI *(d. 939).*

KI TSURAYUKI *(884–946). Held several high offices at Court, culminating in the Governorship of Tosa. Skilled poet, prose writer, and calligrapher. Central figure in the compilation of* Kokinshū *(c. 905), the first Imperial anthology, and author of its Preface. Also compiled* Shinsenwakashū *and author of a diary,* Tosa Nikki.

LADY ISE *(mid tenth century). Daughter of Fujiwara Tsugukage, Governor of Ise. Favourite of Emperor Uda and supposed author of* Yamato Monogatari.

TAIRA KANEMORI *(mid tenth century). Great-grandson of Prince Koretaka, later made Governor of Echigo. One of the 'Thirty-six Poetic Geniuses'.*

ONO KOMACHI *(mid tenth century). One of the 'Six Poetic Geniuses'; served at Court in the fifties of the tenth century.*

KAGURA, *literally 'god-music' (ninth-tenth centuries). The purpose of this performance by dancer, singers, and musicians was to gladden and bid the gods. Details of performances were standardized in the early part of the Heian period and consisted of a dancer who stood in the centre and held a spray of bamboo-grass, a branch of sacred* sakaki, *or a sword; two groups of singers to his left and right who sang in unison, the one group following the other; and an accompanying orchestra of* wagon *(plucked strings), flutes, and percussion.*

AZUMA ASOBI UTA, *literally 'Play-songs of the Eastland'. Folk-songs of the Eastland (present-day Kantō), adopted by the Court, by noble families, and by metropolitan shrines, were regulated as an independent art form by an Imperial Rescript of 920. The Suruga Mai (Suruga Dance) was one of the central pieces in this repertoire and was performed by four or six dancers accompanied by a soloist and chorus and an orchestra of* wagon, *flutes, oboes, and percussion.*

RYŌJIN HISHŌ *(?1179), a collection of songs, in twenty books, by Emperor Go-Shirakawa (1127–92). The three main constituents of the two books of the collection extant are Buddhist hymns, Shintō chants, folk-songs, and traditional songs. Most of the poems are in* Imayō *form, four lines, each of twelve (seven plus five) syllables. In many cases the songs appear to have been handed on by court dancers and singing-girls and by prostitutes.*

HEIKE MONOGATARI, Tale of the Heike *(mid thirteenth century). A war tale, telling the story of the rise and fall of the Heike or Taira clan and its struggles with the Minamoto clan. Originally recited to the accompaniment of the* biwa, *a lute, played by a blind priest.*

IMAYŌ *(literally, 'present mode') from* Heike Monogatari. *Poems of four lines, each line of twelve syllables with a caesura after the seventh, they developed from Buddhist* wasan, *hymns of praise, in the middle years of the Heian period. These 'popular songs in the modern style' were sung by female Court dancers and 'pleasure-girls' and were in frequent use at seasonal festivals and banquets at the Court. Many of the poems are very similar in style and content to those extant in* Ryōjin Hishō.

Kamakura and Muromachi Periods (1185–1603)

TAIRA TADANORI *(1144–84). Younger brother of Kiyomori and a famous soldier, he studied poetry with Shunzei. His poems appear in* Senzaishū *and later Imperial anthologies.*

PRIEST SHUNE *(late twelfth century, fl. 1160–80). Son and poetic heir of Minamoto Toshiyori. Priest of the Tōdaiji at Nara, he took part in many poetic contests.*

PRIEST SAIGYŌ *(1118–90). Entered the priesthood at the age of twenty-three after service in the bodyguard of ex-Emperor Gotoba. Travelled over Japan as an itinerant priest. His poems are collected in a private anthology,* Sankashū.

MUKAI KYORAI *(?1651–1704). Born in Nagasaki and trained as a* samurai *in his youth. Joined Bashō's school 1684–5, edited* Sarumino *with Bonchō and was later regarded by the Bashō school as the authority in the Kansai area.*

NAITŌ JŌSŌ *(1662–1704). A member of the Bashō school.*

HATTORI RANSETSU *(1654–1707). Born in Edo and said, with Kikaku, to be the most gifted of the poets in Bashō's school.*

ENOMOTO KIKAKU *(1661–1707). Born in Edo and ranked, with Ransetsu, as the most gifted of Bashō's disciples. Struck out in the direction of wit and humour after Bashō's death.*

NOZAWA BONCHŌ *(d. 1714). Born in Kanazawa and practised medicine in Kyōto. Entered Bashō's school in the late 1680s and edited* Sarumino *with Kyorai.*

MORIKAWA KYOROKU *(1656–1715). A* samurai *in the service of the Lord of Hikone, he joined the Bashō school from that of Tanaka Tsunenori, an earlier tradition. Also a skilled prose writer and painter.*

YOSA BUSON *(1716–83). Born in Settsu, he learnt his* haiku *in Edo and then moved to Kyōto. He made the greatest contribution to the new developments in* haiku *in the late eighteenth century (the* Temmei *Restoration).*

ŌSHIMA RYŌTA *(1718–87). Born in Shinano, he moved to Edo and soon gathered a large group of disciples (said to number three thousand) which constituted a rival school to that of Kikaku.*

TAKAI KITŌ *(1741–89). Born in Kyōto and a member of Buson's school.*

KATŌ GYŌDAI *(1732–92). Earlier in the service of the shōgunal house in Edo, he retired to devote himself to* haiku *and was the main force in Kyōto in the restoration of* haikai.

TAKAKUWA RANKŌ *(1726–98). A Kanazawa merchant who worked to bring a revival of the* Genroku *style.*

ŌTOMO ŌEMARU *(1722–1805). Owner of a wholesale business in Ōsaka and a disciple of Ryōta. Skilled in* haiku, kyōka, *painting, and calligraphy.*

KOBAYASHI ISSA (*1763–1827*). *Having lost his mother at the age of three, he lived a life of misery under a stepmother whom he detested; his sympathy with suffering and feeling for the underdog are often expressed in his haiku. His frequent use of colloquialism and dialect gives a distinctive character to his poems.*

BASHŌ, KYORAI, BONCHŌ, FUMIKUNI. *Haikai, a series of linked verses, begins with a hokku, a 'long' verse of three lines (of five, seven, and five syllables) and thereafter 'short' (of two lines of seven syllables) and 'long' verses alternate. From the time of Bashō the earlier norm of a series in a hundred verses gave place to a standard length of thirty-six verses. The form originated early in the sixteenth century.*

CHIKAMATSU MONZAEMON (*1653–1725*). *This michiyuki scene (lovers' journey), in alternating five-syllable and seven-syllable lines, is regarded as one of the most poetic passages in the whole of Japanese puppet or kabuki drama. Tokubei, in love with a prostitute, Ohatsu, is tricked out of the dowry money he is planning to return after refusing a match arranged for him by his uncle. In despair, Tokubei and Ohatsu decide to kill themselves and the michiyuki scene describes their journey to the place they have chosen for their suicide.*

SENRYŪ *(from eighteenth century). Poems in seventeen-syllable form originated by Karai Senryū, 1718–90, a native of Edo. Freed from the restrictions on* haiku, *such as season words, these poems most often employ a colloquial style and satirize human emotions and failings.*

KYŌKA *(eighteenth century). Literally 'mad* waka', *these poems, in* tanka *form, were of humorous tone. In both content and style, kyōka poets were freed from all the restrictions on* tanka. *The poems often poke fun at issues of the times and are often parodies, lightening and omitting all the seriousness of the original. Kyōka flourished in Edo in the last twenty years of the eighteenth century. The best-known poets were Yomo Akara (also known as Shokusanjin) and Yadoya Meshimori.*

RYŌKAN *(1757–1831). Priest of the Zen sect.*

TACHIBANA AKEMI *(1812–68). Tanka poet and 'national scholar', writing in the Manyō style.*

FOLK-SONG. *Most of the folk-song translated here goes back to the Edo period (from the seventeenth century) and is based on a quatrain of seven, seven, seven, and five syllables, in contrast to the odd number of lines, with alternating five and seven syllables, of the literary poetry.*

Modern Period (from 1868)

1. *Tanka*

EMPEROR MEIJI *(1852–1912). Reigned 1868–1912, and reputed to have composed more than a hundred thousand tanka.*

ITŌ SACHIO *(1864–1913). Novelist and tanka poet. A disciple of Shiki, he was connected with Saitō Mokichi in the* Araragi *group.*

MASAOKA SHIKI *(1867–1902). Haiku and* tanka *poet. Founder of the journal* Hototogisu. *Advocating a revival of the* Manyō *spirit, he has deeply affected traditional forms (see also p. 156).*

2. *Haiku*

3. Modern *Senryū*

4. *Shintaishi ('New-Style Poetry')*

TSUCHII BANSUI *(1871–1952). Graduate of Tokyo University, specializing in English. Leading lyricist. Essayist and translator.* Kōjō no tsuki (Moon over the ruined castle*), included in early-twentieth-century middle-school song book, is widely known.*

SHIMAZAKI TŌSON *(1872–1943). Graduate of Meiji Gakuin.* Shintaishi *pioneer and leading romanticist. Co-founder of* Bungakkai *(Literary World).*

KAMBARA ARIAKE *(1876–1952). Leading symbolist, member of* Myōjō *group.*

TAKAMURA KŌTARŌ *(1883–1956). Sculptor and poet. Studied in New York, London and Paris. As poet, moved from tanka to become leading pioneer in colloquial-style 'free' poetry.* Myōjō *and* Subaru *(Pleiades) groups.*

KITAHARA HAKUSHŪ *(1885–1942). Highly regarded for tanka, haiku and children's songs as well as shintaishi. A leading symbolist,* Myōjō *and* Subaru *groups.*

ISHIKAWA TAKUBOKU *(1886–1912). Wrote both tanka (*Myōjō *and* Subaru *groups) and shintaishi: 'socialistic' leanings in later poetry.*

HAGIWARA SAKUTARŌ *(1886–1942). Lyricist, co-founder of the* Shiki *group, and pioneer of colloquial-style 'free' poetry.*

MIKI ROFŪ *(1889–1964). Leading symbolist, contributor to* Mirai *(Future) and experimenter in colloquial-language poems.*

TSUBOI SHIGEJI *(1889–1975). Member of Proletarian Writers League and co-founder of* Aka to Shiro *(Red and Black). Involved in the formation of* Shinnihon Bungakkai *after the Pacific War.*

HORIGUCHI DAIGAKU *(1892–1981). Studied symbolism during a long stay in Europe. Translations of foreign literature were a major influence on* Shōwa-*period literature.*

SAIJŌ YASO *(1892–1970). Graduate of Waseda University, specializing in French. Symbolist and contributor to* Mirai.

SATŌ HARUO *(1892–1964). Lyricist, member of* Myōjō *and* Subaru *groups. Many of his best poems use literary style. Novelist and critic.*

historians and critics of classical and modern Japanese poetry. He continues to exercise a
very great influence on the contemporary Japanese literary stage.

SHIRAISHI KAZUKO *(b. 1931). Born in Vancouver. A graduate of Waseda University,*
specializing in art history, she joined Vou, which was led by Kitasono Katsue, who was in
the centre of Japan's avant garde. Shiraishi maintains a high level of literary activity, in essays,
criticism, translation and public readings in Japan and around the world.

TANIKAWA SHUNTARŌ *(b. 1931). From the* Rekitei *group he joined* Kai *in*
1953. The fresh lyricism of his early poems expresses Japan's new hope, an alternative to
the nihilism of the immediate post-war years. Tanikawa is one of the most widely known
figures of the post-war Japanese literary scene, through the range of his activities in radio,
film and TV and the breadth of his writing – picture books, children's stories, drama
and song lyrics as well as poetry.

NAKAE TOSHIO *(b. 1933). A graduate of Kansai University (in Ōsaka), specializing*
in Japanese literature. After publishing in the Arechi *anthologies, he joined the* Kai
group in 1954.

TAKAHASHI MUTSUO *(b. 1937). Graduate of Fukuoka University of Education.*
Distinctive concept of aesthetics from homosexuality, Christianity and the Greek idea of
beauty. Autobiographical novel and works of criticism as well as shintaishi *poetry.*

Introduction

In the brief general preface I wrote to this anthology back in 1964, I began by saying, 'Poetry is in a real sense a living part of the culture of Japan today.' Though prose fiction, past and present, attracts a larger readership, most Japanese, without much effort, can – and many do – compose traditional poems that, if no more, are at least technically correct. The old forms (the classical thirty-one-syllable *tanka* and the seventeenth-century seventeen-syllable *haiku*) still attract many devoted followers, often members of local *tanka* or *haiku* clubs, publishing their own magazines. The Emperor's long-established poetry prize attracts thousands of entries each New Year.

It is true that nowadays tradition is often neglected or observed at best mechanically and with little original feeling. The old game of 'poem-cards' is still played at New Year, though it is now less widespread than it was. Someone reads the first half of a poem from a thirteenth-century anthology, *A Hundred Verses of a Hundred Poets*, and, in this Oriental version of Snap, from the hundred cards containing the second halves of the poems spread on the floor or on the table, the players choose the appropriate one. The clichés of everyday speech, and many proverbial sayings, can still be traced to famous ancient poems. Traditional poetry has permeated the cultural scene and the Japanese sensibility and continues to be a unifying force.

But this is true only of the traditional forms. Faced with *shintaishi* ('new-style poetry' – a vague but comprehensive term that covers the multitude of twentieth-century 'experiments'), many contemporary Japanese will puzzle away at meanings and admit ignorance or impatience. Even so, the atmosphere is more friendly to the poet than is usual in many places. Poets meet a show of respect which, though it may not always be based on much knowledge, is genial and thoughtful.

Sometimes officialdom and bureaucracy are enlisted to give such respect financial support and public sustenance. When I was invited to read and take part in discussions at the sixteenth so-called 'World Congress of Poets' in August 1996, held in the city of Maebashi, I was astonished to discover that over five hundred Japanese poets (as well as three hundred foreign poets) were attending. The Japanese ranged from devoted traditionalists, many of them members of the clubs I have mentioned, such famous 'new-style' poets as Tanikawa Shuntarō and Shiraishi Kazuko, to much younger experimentalists who followed a variety of modern mentors. All were welcomed by the Mayor of Maebashi, who was proud of the fact that his city was the birthplace of Hagiwara Sakutarō (1886–1942), one of the most important – and innovative – of *shintaishi* writers.

The Mayor of Maebashi may have been slightly unusual in his warm welcome to several hundred poets. But there are other public manifestations of interest in poetry, both old and new. For several years the *Asahi Shimbun*, one of Japan's most respected newspapers, has carried each day (and on the front page) a poem chosen by Ōoka Makoto, a leading living poet and critic. Each poem carries context, explanation, comment. This sort of thing, true, is not entirely unknown in the West: *The New York Times* for a period in the 1960s sporadically published new poems, and more recently the British *Independent* newspaper has followed a policy of publishing each day a 'new' (sometimes old) poem – good, bad or indifferent. But neither had, or has, the impact of Ōoka's carefully chosen poems, from early *tanka* and *haiku* to the newest free verse.

This congenial, serious, devoted attitude comes from a very long poetical history, as Geoffrey Bownas makes clear in his own Introduction. One looks through poems written over a period of more than a thousand years and finds how the same themes and even the same images recur. The wild geese were watched in the seventh century as they flew north in the early spring, and in the twentieth century

> Undergraduates,
> By and large shabby:
> Wild geese flying off.

Any important event in life may stir the Japanese poet, but above all it is nature that has been the chief inspirer. The Japanese in general have the notion that man is not only part of nature but that the two are one – and this even now, when the vast majority of the population live in urban places, including huge conurbations. Much of Japan is still mountainous, wild, unsettleable. The unmelted snow in spring, the cherry blossom; summer fireflies or morning glory; autumn's harvest moon, its red maple leaves and the first chill winds; the hailstorms and withered fields of winter – all these have been the inspiration of Japanese poetry, and they can still be found today, however startlingly readjusted.

Over the ages, the dominant characteristic of much Japanese poetry has been its gentle melancholy, its sense of *mono no aware* (which a Roman poet, without knowing Japanese, called *lacrimae rerum*). The great sadness at the heart of things, the sad lessons of transience that nature teaches us, the quiet pleasures of solitude – all these can be found in the poems of the first anthology of the eighth century AD and in many recent slim volumes. Yet at these two extremes of time, one can find other, sometimes more pressingly urgent things, equally representative of the complex Japanese personality: the tough stoicism of some of the early frontier guards' poems; Ōtomo Yakamochi's squib *Making fun of a thin man* (also from the eighth century); the violence, sensuality, satirical edge and restless eclecticism of much modern work.

The Japanese poet has traditionally been devoted to hints, suggestions, an image-laden obliquity; he leaves out all inessentials. In this he is like his fellow painter or potter, who aims for ellipsis, brevity and the aesthetic quality known as *shibui* – something astringent, muted, indirect, even rough, though held within the bounds of artistic decorum. In the mid twentieth century, and particularly in the short-lived 'proletarian' school of poets, many readers found something too brash, too well defined, too outspoken: they recoiled from direct statements and forthright outbursts. But more recently, it seems, styles coexist, and the modernist lion can lie down with the traditionalist lamb. Examples of this coexistence can be found towards the end of this revised anthology.

From the beginning of our work back in the 1950s, Geoffrey Bownas and I have been keen to show that behind the traditional forms, and together with them, lies a great mass of folk poetry, the voice of Anon: planting songs, lullabies, *Bon* festival lyrics and an endless number of *senryū* – those humorous, deflationary, sharp-eyed little poems written in the same seventeen-syllable form as the *haiku*, but substituting realism, even satire, for fancy, whimsy or the transcendental:

> A horse farts;
> Four or five suffer
> On the ferry-boat.

In my 1964 preface I observed, 'It is perhaps among these unpretentious pieces that the Western reader will feel most quickly at home. We have therefore given more space to anonymous poetry and folk poetry than a Japanese might think proper.' Today, this seems unnecessarily hedging, indeed probably untrue. The Japanese are aware, and indeed proud, of their anonymous folk tradition, both historically and anthropologically.

Finally, I have to acknowledge that the English-speaking readership of this late 1990s updating and revision of our anthology is probably very different from the one we approached in the mid 1960s. In the years that followed the 1964 version, there can have been few schools in the United States, Britain, Australia and elsewhere which did not see occasional flurries of *haiku* writing in English, encouraged by teachers who, flushed with a little learning, were keen to inspire their pupils with brief lessons from 'the world of dew'. They were no doubt themselves encouraged by the example of such eminent poets as W. H. Auden and the Greek Nobel Prizewinner, George Seferis, who were moved to make 'imitations' of Japanese poems, if not translations of translations, soon after the 1964 Penguin book appeared. Today, Japanese poetry is far more familiar outside Japan than it was when Geoffrey Bownas and I first went to work. But it is high time that we brought our book up to date.

For help and advice, I thank the following: Tanikawa Shuntarō, Shiraishi Kazuko, Takahashi Yasunari, Yamanouchi Hisaaki, Yaman-ouchi Reiko.

Anthony Thwaite
September 1998

A Short History of Japanese Poetry

1. The Language

Little can be said with any certainty about the origins and affinities of the Japanese language. There are structural similarities with Korean and other members of the Ural–Altaic group, but these are not supported by identities in vocabulary; on the other hand, while such identities occur between Japanese and the languages of the islands to the south and south-east, there is hardly any evidence of structural affinity.

Whatever the origins of the Japanese language, it is well known that there was no indigenous script, and it was only with the adoption of the Chinese character (probably early in the fifth century AD) that Japan came to possess a literary tradition. The effects of this loan were far-reaching and we shall see some of them in the course of this survey of the history of Japanese verse. Not least among them was the fact that thenceforth literate Japanese might always be able to read Chinese and keep abreast of new literary currents in China; at the same time, the more sensitive among them would be for ever conscious of a certain cultural indebtedness to their elder brothers on the Asiatic mainland.

This borrowing, one of the first of a long list of Japan's cultural and material loans, was as ingenious as any that followed. For the Japanese might adopt a Chinese character in one of two ways. First, it could serve as a semantic, a means of setting down the sense of the original Japanese word. This was all very well as long as the linguistic habits of borrower and creditor coincided, as they did in the case of the noun, which is indeclinable and invariable as to number in both languages. But with the transcription of, say, the adjective or the verb, the Japanese were faced with a much more complex problem. Classical Chinese is uninflected and lacks parts of speech. In their highly flexional language, Japanese grammarians distinguish three categories: indeclinables; 'working words', i.e. adjectives and verbs which are capable of flexion ('work'); and particles, which are postpositional and either (when following a noun) indicate its grammatical relation to its context, or (when ending the clause or sentence) serve as aids to the expression of exclamation, emphasis, doubt, certainty, and so on. (They are, obviously, of great value to the poet who has thus a rich field of choice instead of 'oh!' and 'ah!'.)

The second function of the Chinese character, as a phonetic, was to solve the problem of the adaptation of the script of an uninflected language to meet the demands and record the flexional variants of a language very rich in flexion. This might be achieved in several ways; for example, the semantic root of the Japanese word might be written in its Chinese equivalent, with additional characters, used purely for their phonetic value and regardless of their semantic content, appended as a means of recording the flexional suffixes to this semantic root. (Since Chinese was monosyllabic and Japanese polysyllabic, each Japanese syllable had to be given its individual Chinese character equivalent in this phonetic game.)

The earliest Japanese literary work extant, *Kojiki* (*Record of Ancient Matters*, completed AD 712), employs both systems of transcription. The compiler was apparently quite aware of the nature of the problems that faced him, for he wrote in his Preface: 'To make exclusive use of characters [i.e. used semantically] would involve problems of meaning; to record entirely by the phonetic method would lengthen my account unduly. Hence I sometimes employ both phonetic and semantic systems in the same passage or sometimes use the latter exclusively.'

The phonetic method was used in *Kojiki* in the contexts with which we are particularly concerned, in poems and songs, for instance, and for the transcription of proper nouns such as place and personal names. In these contexts, the compiler wished to reproduce native words and felt that sinification would weaken the force of native Japanese.

Kojiki was soon followed by another chronicle, *Nihon Shoki* (*Chronicle of Japan*, AD 720). Here the debt to China is even more apparent for, with the exception of the songs which are transcribed phonetically, Chinese is employed throughout, with not even any attempt at preserving Japanese constructions. Where the original *Kojiki* uses the indigenous sacred number eight (as in 'eight-forked serpent'), the number is frequently changed to the seven or nine favoured by the Chinese in parallel passages in *Nihon Shoki*.

By the time of the compilation of the first great anthology of poetry to come down to us, *Manyōshū* (*Collection of a Myriad Leaves*), the Japanese were becoming more skilled in the phonetic use of the Chinese character. The collection was compiled in the late Nara period, the latter part of the eighth century. A study of the dated poems shows that, by and large, while the Chinese character was used semantically until the end of the seventh century, poems from the mid eighth century onwards are written phonetically. Characters so used came to be known by the term *kana* – 'borrowed names' or 'nouns loaned'.

There was at first no standardization or limitation in the choice of such *kana* from a vast potential field of homonymous Chinese characters. However, by the middle of the ninth century, the range of characters used as phonetic symbols had been considerably narrowed and the original Chinese character drastically simplified and abbreviated. As a result, the act of reading became less awesome and that of writing less time-consuming.

As Japanese writers grew more and more proficient in the use of this auxiliary *kana* script, they were able to make themselves increasingly independent of Chinese. Certain circumstances of the tenth century (Japan no longer sent embassies to a China that was in sorry disunion after the collapse of the T'ang dynasty) favoured the growth of a native tradition in prose as well as poetry (where most attempts to get away from Chinese had been made hitherto). Ki Tsurayuki, whose Preface to the first Imperial anthology, *Kokinshū* (*Collection of Poems Ancient and Modern*) we shall discuss at some length later, wrote *c.* 935, entirely in *kana*, *Tosa Nikki* (*Tosa Diary*), notes on the details of a journey back to the capital from the province of Tosa. In that it is written in *kana*, the diary purports to come from the hand of the wife of the provincial Governor – Tsurayuki did, in fact, serve as Governor of Tosa – and the reason Tsurayuki gives for this early act of literary dumping is that he, a man, would have flouted convention unless he composed in Chinese.

xlvi   A SHORT HISTORY OF JAPANESE POETRY

Indeed, the development of native letters was by no means univer-
sal. Japanese did not lend itself to certain genres for which Chinese
was preferred, and there was always the price of the snob value, in
the case of a man, of flaunting his ability to compose both prose and
verse in Chinese. Some of these attempts were of the level of the
schoolboy Latin exercise; but there were scholars who had a genuine
feel for Chinese and had the benefit of long years of study in China.
That the urge to compose in Chinese was not by any means confined
to the few is shown by the fact that it was possible to compile
anthologies of Chinese verse written by Japanese. The first of these,
Kaifūsō (Fond Recollections of Poetry), came out in 751, antedating
Manyōshū, and contained material from the latter part of the seventh
century.

Some of the features of the language conditioned the development
of Japanese verse. First, the nature of the adjective. Japanese gram-
marians classify the adjective along with the verb as a 'working word'.
In most Indo-European languages the adjective is closely related
to and governed by the noun it qualifies, whether attributively or
predicatively. Much of our linguistic experience leads us to make the
link adjective—noun in the matter of case, number, or gender flexions.
But it is not relevant for the Japanese adjective that there is no
nominal flexion that will specify any of these three factors, for the
adjective acts in a manner much more akin to that of the verb and
frequently stands duty for the verb in that it is really a fusion of
adjective and copula. In fact, the adjective conjugates!

The purpose of conjugation again comes as something of a surprise
to one whose experience is restricted to Indo-European languages.
For whereas the primary function of conjugation in the latter is to
specify the time at which the action or state in the verb occurs (e.g.
present, future, preterite), its purpose in Japanese is concerned rather
with the degree of doubt or certainty in the action of the verb or the
quality of the adjective. To keep to terms with which we are familiar,
Japanese conjugation is a matter perhaps more of mood than of tense.

A few examples will clarify this assertion. First, from present-day
Japanese: the verbal suffix *-mai*, for instance, has the force of 'probably
will not' and derives from a fusion of a future auxiliary *mu* in its
non-effected form *ma*, with *ji*, a negative suffix. The suffix *-tai* is a

desiderative added to a modified verbal root which itself acts as an adjective and is capable of assuming most verbal and adjectival 'workings'. Secondly, examples of verbal and adjectival flexion in classical Japanese. The last line, 'At which I gaze so long', in Narihira's poem (p. 71),

> Tossing in my bed
> The whole night through,
> Neither waking nor sleeping,
> It is a thing of spring,
> This long rain haze
> At which I gaze so long

is an attempt to render a compound verb *nagame-kurashi-tsu* which alone occupies the seven syllables of the last line in the Japanese. *Nagame-kurashi* is 'to live looking at' and the final syllable *-tsu* is an affirmative suffix. Adjectives, too, are capable of a wide variety of flexion; *nodokekaramashi*, which again constitutes the whole of a seven-syllable line, is formed by suffixing *-mashi* – indicating a future probability, often with a force of volition, 'would' or 'would like to' – to the imperfect base of an adjective-verb *nodokeki*, 'tranquil'; the meaning is 'would have been tranquil'.

It will be clear that such an involved flexional structure is very suitable as a tool for the lyric poet. With such aids, tone and mood can be suggested with fine delicacy and states of mind dissected and described in close detail. If the whole of the linguistic experience of the Japanese moulds him to express himself in terms such as 'I probably shall not think so,' conjecture and imagination appear as second nature in poetry. To the Japanese poet, it has always seemed preferable to suggest in vague terms, to hint, to symbolize, rather than to express fully and plainly.

2. *Prosody*

Before we examine the rules of Japanese prosody we must discuss certain other features of the language. The basis of the phoneme is the *kana* syllable which consists invariably of either a single vowel or consonant and vowel; the modern *n* alone, a seeming exception, has lost a final *u*. Thus there can be no consonantal clusters and even where, in the voicing of a foreign word, there appears to be consonantal reduplication, in reality the Japanese will write such clusters by means of distinct *kana* symbols and will separate them when he is counting syllables. So, for example, the Chinese word *hatten* is not two syllables, *hat* and *ten*, but four – *ha-tu-te-n*; and *programme* or *blacklist* become *pu-ro-gu-ra-mu* and *bu-ra-tu-ku-ri-su-to*, juxtaposed consonants thus suffering the insertion of a separating vowel, most frequently *u*, the weakest of the five (*a, i, u, e* and *o*). In that the syllable always ends in one of the five vowels, rhyme becomes so simple and monotonous as to be pointless. Again, in that each syllable is given equal quantity, whether consisting of simple vowel or consonant and vowel, and in that there are no sounds, in pure Japanese at least, where a glottal hesitation on a consonantal reduplication or a hovering on the richness of a diphthong offers variety in either sound or syllable length, there is an absence of such features as might lead the Japanese poet to add to his basic rule of prosody, a syllable count.

Because of the nature of our sources for primitive song and early poetry (both *Kojiki* and *Nihon Shoki* incorporated material that had gone through a long period of oral tradition and was no doubt worked over when it was reduced to writing) it is hard to assign a precise date to the appearance of a fixed syllabic prosody and a regular form.

The line length in the poems and songs preserved in *Kojiki* and *Nihon Shoki* (and again in the early poems in *Manyōshū*) varies between three and nine syllables, although even at this early stage there are hints of a preference for five or seven syllables. Thus, the first poem in *Manyōshū*, by Emperor Yūryaku (418–79), begins with lines of three, four, five and six syllables (p. 7):

> *Ko mo yo*
> *Miko mochi*   With her basket, her basket (lines 1–2)
> *Fugushi mo yo*   And her trowel, her trowel (lines 3–4)
> *Mibugushi mochi*

(a pattern of increase not paralleled elsewhere in the poem).

There is a similar absence of syllabic pattern to match the parallelism in sound and sense in a poem in *Kojiki* in praise of the Palace of Hishiro (p. 5):

Makimuku no	(5) At Makimuku
Hishiro no miya wa	(7) The Palace of Hishiro
Asahi no	(4) Basks in
Hideru miya	(5) The daytime sun,
Yūhi no	(4) Flashes in
Higakeru miya	(6) The evening sun . . .

Many of these early songs are so irregular in form as to defy division into lines or stanzas.

However, by the time of the composition of the great majority of the poems in *Manyōshū*, song had developed into poem, poem with a determined line length and regular forms. The line is invariably of five or seven syllables, short and long lines alternating; for example, Prince Arima's poem on preparing for a journey (p. 8):

Iwashiro no	(5) On the beach of Iwashiro
Hamamatsu ga e wo	(7) I pull and knot together
Hikimusubi	(5) The branches of the pine.
Masakiku araba	(7) If my fate turns out well,
Mata kaerimimu	(7) I shall return to see them again.

This form, of thirty-one syllables in five lines of five, seven, five, seven and seven, is by far the most common and persistent of the three that had developed by the time of *Manyōshū*; it still survives — by no means precariously — today. It is the *tanka*, 'short poem', or *waka*, 'Japanese poem', form. The other two forms are again constituted from five-syllable or seven-syllable lines. The *sedōka*, of which there are only about sixty examples, of a total of well over four thousand poems in the anthology, is a six-line form, consisting of a double tercet of five, seven and seven syllables. There is an example in a poem from *Kokashū* (*Collection of Ancient Poems*), an early collection by an unknown compiler which was incorporated into *Manyōshū* (p. 16):

Tama-dare no	(5) Through the chinks
Osu no sukeki ni	(7) Of the jewelled blinds

Iri-kayoi ko ne	(7) Come to me.
Tarachine no	(5) Should my mother ask –
Haha ga towasaba	(7) Mother of the sagging breasts –
Kaze to mōsamu	(7) I'll say it was the wind.

The *sedōka* form disappeared even sooner than the *chōka*, 'long poem', the third of the forms in *Manyōshū*, and, like the *tanka*, consisting of alternate lines of five and seven syllables with an additional final seven-syllable line. There was no limit on the length of the *chōka* form – the longest in *Manyōshū* does not exceed 150 lines – and it might be rounded off by one, two or even more *hanka*, 'repeat poems' or 'envoys', which are in *tanka* form and generally elaborate on or summarize the theme of the main poem.

Although the *chōka* form flourished in the first part of the eighth century (the years of Hitomaro, p. 22f. and Okura, p. 32f.), it was very rarely employed after the end of the Manyō period. In spite of the obvious dexterity of its most inspired exponents, and the sustention and richness they achieved, the form was clearly one in which the less saintly poet was below his best. The *chōka* of the later Manyō period are little more than skimpingly poetic prose and show, by comparison with the *tanka* of the time, the tendency of the Japanese to abuse the freedoms of a longer form.

The decline of the *chōka* is often interpreted in terms of the lack of sustaining power in the Japanese writer. Thus, the prose writer is happiest of all when he employs a form which falls readily into short and unrelated episodic sections, such as the literary diary, the collection of *belles-lettres* or the short story. So, one of the earliest prose works, *Ise Monogatari* (*The Tales of Ise*), is a loose sequence of independent prose passages which set the scene of and act as headnotes for Narihira's poems (p. 67f), while the twentieth-century novel frequently lacks cohesion and in some hands is little more than a series of short stories or novelettes, each chapter complete in itself.

This explanation of the decline of the *chōka* is not quite the whole answer, for, whether or not the Japanese poet realized the infelicities that arose when he composed in longer forms, there is an occasional yet quite persistent hankering after means of writing at greater length and with a deal more cohesion than could have been effected by a series of *tanka*. So, for example, *Kagerō Nikki*, a late-tenth-century diary, contains its *chōka*; the *renga* (linked-verse) form which dates from the fourteenth century could be seen in part as an attempt to break through the limitations imposed by *tanka* form; whole passages of drama, in particular the chorus sections in the *Nō* and scenes in puppet or *kabuki* drama (p. 121f. *The Love Suicides at Sonezaki*) are in *chōka* form; the *haikai* of the Edo period (p. 118f. *The Kite's Feathers*) is a linked-verse series, while sequences such as *Poems on the Kema Dyke in the Spring Breeze*, written by Buson in 1777, link *haiku* and Chinese poems.

In addition to this characteristic of the Japanese poet when composing in longer forms, it seems that further factors peculiar to the period hastened the decline of the *chōka*. Certain of these influences will be more apparent when we have discussed more fully the topics that inspired the Japanese poet and the circumstances in which and purposes for which he wrote. In brief, Japanese poetry tended more and more in the Manyō period to settle into the lyrical and private, informal mode which was to characterize the *tanka* for the rest of its long lifetime. By the time of Akahito (d. 736?, p. 38), there are visible the beginnings of a tendency both to shorten the *chōka* quite drastically and to channel all the poetic art into the 'envoys' which often effect no integral link with the preceding *chōka* or each other. The *chōka* thus came more and more to act as a palely poetic headnote, detailing the circumstances or the sources of the poetic inspiration of the *tanka* which followed. The culmination of the process was the *uta-monogatari* ('poem-tale') like *Ise Monogatari* (? late ninth century) or again the literary diary where, in a similar way, poems acquired prose contexts.

In addition, the later years of the Manyō period corresponded with the poetic heights of T'ang China attained by Li Po (701–62), Tu Fu (712–70) and Po Chü-i (772–846). The overawing influence of China was again at work, and for the century following the end of the Manyō period, by far the greater part of the poet's energy was spent in frantic pursuit of the fashion of the day, composition in Chinese. If a man were bitten by the poetic bug, and particularly if the bite went so deep as to require him to compose at length, he eased the hurt by writing a Chinese poem. By and large, Japanese poetry was relegated to female brushes, except when the male-biting bug was of the love variety, requiring him to write a *tanka* for the object of his passion. Perhaps, through this lean period, the *tanka* owed no small part of its continued existence to the fact that the process of love-making demanded in the courtier at least a nodding acquaintance with the rules of *tanka* composition.

In this discussion we have anticipated some of the more important later developments in form. To restate them briefly: first, the alternation of lines of five and seven syllables remained the basis of practically all Japanese poetry until the modern period. Even the *imayō*, 'present mode', which developed in the middle Heian period and was a type of popular song in 'modern style', sung by court dancers and courtesans or used at seasonal festivals, adheres to the mould. *Imayō* are in four lines, each of twelve syllables, which break down into units of seven and five with a caesura after the seventh. Thus (p. 86):

> *Furuki miyako wo / kite mireba*
> *Asazahara tozo / arenikeru*
> *Tsuki no hikari wa / kuma nakute*
> *Akikaze nomi zo / mi ni wa shimu*
> We come and we see the capital of old,
> Desolate as a swamp unkempt with wild reeds.
> The light of the moon streams in unshaded:
> The wind of autumn pierces my bones.

The *kouta*, 'little ballad' (as distinct from the court ballad or poem) of the Muromachi period was a fifteenth- and sixteenth-century continuation of the Heian *imayō* form and, like that form, was meant to be sung. So, from *Kanginshū* (1518) we have (p. 101):

> *Tsuki wa yamada no / ue ni ari*
> *Fune wa akashi no / oki wo kogu . . .*
> The moon shines over the hill field:
> His boat puts out to sea off Akashi . . .

But the folk form, *dodoitsu*, eschews this alternation, for the line division of its twenty-six syllables is seven, seven, seven and five. Thus (p. 143):

Bon ni odoro ka	'Are you dancing in the *Bon*?'
Kotoshi no bon ni ya	'Yes – because this year
Hara ni ko wa nashi	There's no babe in my belly
Mi wa karoshi	And I feel light as air.'

and

Akai yumoji ni	Anyone not tempted out
Madowanu mono wa	By the red loincloths of *Bon*
Kibutsu kanabutsu	Is a Buddha made of wood or bronze,
Ishi botoke	A Buddha made of stone.

The very existence of the *tanka* form today, well over a thousand years after its origin, bears witness to its appropriateness to the Japanese poetic mentality. But this is not to say that this form of Japanese poetry has not undergone considerable internal development. One of the most important changes is the transition in the position of the caesuras or pauses in the syntax. In the Manyō period, the great majority of *tanka* have such pauses after the second and fourth lines, the poem thus being divisible into units of five and seven (twelve), five and seven (twelve) and seven, a top-heavy pattern which fails to escape from the simple alternation of a shorter followed by a longer line and, except in the most skilled hands, tends to lose its force in the final short unit. Thus (p. 27):

Hayabito no	Clear and loud	(line 3)
Na ni ou yogoe	As the night call	(2)
Ichishiroku	Of a man of Haya,	(1)
Waga na wa noritsu	I told my name.	(4)
Tsuma to tanomase	Trust me as your wife.	(5)

and, by Lady Kasa in the eighth century (p. 54):

Yaoya yuku	Even the grains of sand	(line 2)
Hama no masago mo	On a beach eight hundred days wide	(1–2)
Waga koi ni	Would not be more than my love,	(3–4)
Ani masarajika	Watchman of the island coast.	(5)
Okitsushima mori		

On the other hand, in the *tanka* of the Heian and Kamakura periods, the caesuras often fall at the end of the first and third lines, thus dividing the poem into three units of increasing length, five, twelve and fourteen syllables. Thus, in a poem of Narihira in *Ise Monogatari* (p. 67):

Tsuki ya aranu	Can it be that the moon has changed?
Haru ya mukashi no	Can it be that the spring
Haru naranu	Is not the spring of old times?
Waga mi hitotsu wa	Is it my body alone
Moto no mi nishite	That is just the same?

Here, both caesuras are marked by conclusive verbs (*aranu*, *naranu*) and the close link between the second and third lines, the middle unit, is established by the possessive particle *no*; line four, the first part of the final and longest section, is the subject of the verb at the end of line five.

It is not simply that this pattern of growth is more pleasing and powerful in itself; in addition, the new division facilitated the poet's escape from a distich pattern with the shorter line invariably as the first element. This new breakdown, involving a central unit where the seven-syllable line was the first constituent, no doubt fostered the development of the *imayō* style, where the twelve-syllable line has a caesura after the seventh syllable. Much more important, in that the second caesura is stronger than the first, this later style of *tanka* might be said to break down into two main parts, the first three and the last two lines (seventeen: fourteen syllables). From this division there came first the linked-verse form, *renga*, where the first stanza is of three lines, the second two, the third three lines again and so on, and then *haiku*, in form at any rate the equivalent of this first main unit of the *tanka*.

The Japanese shares some of his prosodic techniques with poets of other cultures. The high incidence of vowels and the incisive cleanness of the single consonant make assonance and alliteration highly effective. Certain vowels and consonants are conventionally associated with specifically defined moods and tones. Thus, in employing assonance and alliteration, the Japanese poet is able to count on a more ready response to the atmosphere for which he is aiming than can, at least, his English counterpart. The repetition of the vowel *o* often gives an effect of dullness, obscurity or profundity, as in *honobono to*, dimly, vaguely, or *oboro-zuki*, the pale, clouded moon. *U* is also a vowel which carries a sense of vagueness. *A* denotes clarity or splendour, as in the phrase *akanesasu*, which acts as a 'pillow-word', a conventional epithet, to the sun or the moon or to the verb 'to shine'; or as in *tamamokaru*, 'where the gem-seaweed is cut', a 'pillow-word' for the sea-shore, the name of a bay or a place on the sea.

Alliteration by the repetition of *k*, for example, may give an effect of melancholy as in Bashō's *haiku* (p. 105):

Kare eda ni	On a bare branch
Karasu no tomarikeri	A rook roosts:
Aki no kure	Autumn dusk.

Alliteration of *s* conveys softness or tenderness, the dentals signify the sense of the eternal or the all-powerful and *h* contains a suggestion of bloom or expansion, as in

Haru no hatsu hana   The flowers that bloom in the spring.

The links between sound and mood are illustrated further in relation to Bashō's *haiku* below (pp. lxvii–lxviii).

From the first, the Japanese poet shows himself aware of the art of both phonetic and syntactic parallelism. In that the *kana* monosyllable, which is often independent or semi-independent, is the unit of scansion, and as complex sounds consisting of diphthongs and consonantal clusters do not appear, phonetic parallelism, which can also draw on an abundance of homonyms, is at once easy to achieve and highly effective.

It is employed in the first poem in *Manyōshū*:

Ko mo yo
Miko mochi
Fugushi mo yo
Mibugushi mochi.

The Palace of Hishiro abounds in parallel lines, words, and phrases:

> *Asahi no*
> *Hideru miya*
> *Yūhi no*
> *Higakeru miya*
> *Take no ne no*
> *Nedaru miya*
> *Ko no ne no*
> *Nebau miya* (lines 3–10)

and the parallelism of the central section of this poem is too explicit to require comment (p. 5. 'Its topmost branches . . .').

Okura's *The impermanence of human life* (p. 36) is a complex web of phonetic, semantic and structural parallelism.

However, the Japanese poet also made use of certain prosodic techniques which are less familiar. The most generally employed of these is the *makura kotoba*, the 'pillow-word', which is a qualifier describing, by convention, certain nouns or concepts. In that, like all qualifiers in Japanese, it precedes the term it qualifies, the latter rests its head on it as on a pillow. Since nearly all pillow-words or terms are in five syllables, their frequent use may have been in part responsible for the early reluctance to break the sense between the lines of a five-seven couplet, which, as we have seen, was not overcome until it became practice in Heian period *tanka* to place the caesuras after the first and third lines, both of which are of five syllables.

The pillow-word has often been likened to the Homeric stock epithet, but this comparison fails to do full justice to its essence and purpose. There is often an alliterative or assonantal ring in a pillow-word (for example, *akanesasu*, p. lv), which assists its basic task, that of so decorating the word qualified that the reader is made to pause on the latter. Further, in that many of the head-words are place names, it is suggested that part of the purpose of the pillow-word in its early use in a primitive society was to act as a talisman for the good fortune of the place in question. It is as if one wrote:

> Belting along the –
> Heaven-preserve-it –
> M25

> And not crossing –
> God-help-it –
> Oxford Circus.

This magical element in the pillow-word was of less relevance to a more advanced society so that, as primitive song developed into poetry proper, the pillow-word became rather less generally used.

Some pillow-words had an imagistic function; 'black as fish's bowels' (*mina no wata*) of a woman's hair, or 'black as the leopard-flower' (*nubatama no*) of the night, clearly belong to this category. Others appear to have no sense-content and to be used as auditory metaphor. The sense of some is immediately apparent, some require a deal of commentary, some again are still to be explained. Thus *kusa makura*, 'grass for pillow' as a bolster for the head-word 'journey' is eminently clear; but to understand why *akitsu shima*, 'island of the dragonfly' should qualify Yamato, one must know that when a dragonfly's tail touches its mouth and its body forms a ring, this ring is like that created round the plain of Yamato by an almost unbroken circle of mountains (p. 7, *Climbing Mount Kagu*).

The almost complete disappearance of the *chōka* in the Heian period was no doubt in part the cause of the less extensive use of the pillow-word; the *tanka* was already brief enough and it would be spendthrift to squander a whole line on such decoration. On the other hand, another prosodic technique, that of the *kake-kotoba*, pivot-word, became more valuable as the *tanka* became the norm, for it facilitated an added richness of texture. The technique is to employ a single word in a pivotal position between two clauses, in such a way that it is constructed in two different senses; the pivot-word thus acts as a two-way hinge, shifting in sense and, by this shift, linking two images. It is as if one wrote, to give a laboured example,

> Here in our old home/I gaze at the tall pine/[Pine] not for me, my
>   love.

This technique was facilitated by the paucity of phonemes in Japanese and the consequent wide variety and large number of homonyms.

3. Poetic Subjects and Styles

Until the establishment of a permanent capital at Nara in AD 710, the court had moved – within Yamato – with the accession of each sovereign, probably to evade the pollution generated by the death of the sovereign's predecessor. The avoidance of physical or ritual pollution, one of the principal tenets of Shintō, the indigenous religion, has always been a powerful spring of action in Japan. But, however mean or primitive what preceded it, the metropolis of Nara was indeed an achievement. Relations with China at the time were close; officials, students and traders sailed regularly and brought back detailed accounts of all they saw. As a result, Nara was a replica of the T'ang capital with its system of planned, chequer-board streets and boulevards (p. 83, 'the broad walks of Nara'). Vast wooden buildings were raised and a bronze image of the Buddha, fifty-three feet tall, was successfully cast in 749 after many failures. As happened on later occasions, Japan seemed to discover in herself a sprightly vitality as a result of contacts with the outside world. The spirit of the culture of the Nara period, its art, its architecture and its sculpture, as well as its poetry, is summed up by the Japanese by the taste-word *makoto*, literally, 'sincerity'. If 'sincerity' can be taken in the sense of *naïveté*, an artless effusion of pure, sensuous feeling, then the term is eminently appropriate. The spirit of bustling vitality is well caught in a poem in *Manyōshū*:

> The spring has come, the spring
> That wakens the fern's buds
> Above the waterfall
> That wets the rocks with spray.

In spite of the traditional Japanese claim that the *Manyōshū* poets represent a broad sweep through all the social levels in Nara society 'from Emperor to serving-girl, from Minister of State to fisherman or soldier', it seems more proper to regard these poems as the product of a cultivated aristocratic group centred on the capital. Most of the better known poets, such as Tabito, Okura and Yakamochi, served the state, and many of these have recourse to the trick of using other social classes as their mouthpiece. So Okura speaks through the lips of the fisherman (*Poems of the fisherfolk of Shika*, p. 32) and Yakamochi (p. 61) speaks for the departing frontier guard, posted to serve under the authority in Kyūshū (*Dazaifu*) which had charge of coastal defence in the event of an incursion from the Asiatic mainland. In only one case, that of the *Azuma Uta* (*Poems from the Eastland*, p. 20), can we be reasonably certain that we are not being offered something deeply influenced or edited almost beyond recognition by the urban poets: here, local variants, vowel slips (the switch from *a* to *e*, for example) and dialect terms not in general circulation seem to offer proof of provincial provenance. The same is true of some of the *Poems by Frontier Guards* (pp. 51–3) although this is a genre dear to the heart of the metropolitan poet.

Nature, love, partings and time were the subjects that engaged the Manyō poet most. The contrast of past with present and the preoccupation with change occur constantly; and there are the first hints of the influence of Buddhism (which was to grow and leave its mark deep on nearly all Japanese poetry) in the expressions, most frequent and eloquent in Okura's *chōka*, of a resigned sadness in face of inexorable change in this world. Thus, in the *Dialogue on poverty* (p. 36):

> Is this the way things go?
> Must it go on and on?
> Yes. We are on earth.
> Earth is despair and shame.
> But I am no bird, and I
> Cannot escape from it.

And from *The impermanence of human life* (p. 36):

> We are helpless in this world.
> The years and months slip past
> Like a swift stream, which grasps and drags us down.

and later:

> We grudge life moving on
> But we have no redress.

I would become as those
Firm rocks that see no change.
But I am a man in time
And time must have no stop.

Okura was one of the few whose experience in China generated a Confucian conscience or an awareness of the didactic function of poetry. And it is in his verse that we see some of the first signs of the trend towards increased personal lyricism which grew more obvious at the end of the Nara period.

The spirit of the Heian period, named after the new capital Heian (City of Peace; the modern Kyōto) to which the court moved in 794, is best characterized by the taste-word most often applied to its cultural products, *miyabi*. *Miyabi* implies courtly elegance, decorous taste, the nobles' innate faculty of avoiding the ugly, the unclean, the inappropriate.

The age was that of the manorial system with the great Fujiwara clan as the principal manor holder. The Fujiwara gained control of the two great offices of state and, over a long period, retained the privilege of selecting the Empress from their clan. The tone of Heian literature in the tenth and early eleventh centuries was something that could have been set only by such a narrow circle of court nobles, self-assured, urbane and witty, living beyond all threat of war in one of the largest capitals in the world.

This court circle had eyes for little beyond its own kind; it had its own aristocratic Buddhist sect, Shingon, the True Word, designed for an age when all is well with the world, when there is little occasion to seek solace from your god. This metropolitan society took delight in and placed great weight on the arts of music, the dance, calligraphy, painting and poetry. It is very evident from the *Diaries* and *Tales* (*monogatari*) of the period that not only formal occasions, such as leave-taking or the important stages in a love affair, but many ordinary, everyday circumstances called for verse-making. In this sense, poetry was still very much alive and functional in daily living; this natural quality, or at least a channelled natural outpouring, was to be lost when the poet became more self-critical and when the making of poetry came to be a much more ritualized and formal activity.

Even so, the *tanka* poetry of the Heian period was far more self-conscious and trammelled than had been the 'sincere' outpourings of the Manyō age. The stress on taste and refinement involved fining down all inelegance and ousting all crudity from poetry. Hence, for instance, the pillow-word 'black as fish's bowels' fell into disuse and the unconventional departures of poets such as Sone Yoshitada (pp. xiv, 81) earned ostracism from the court poetic circle. Convention came to govern the poet in his choice of theme as well as the diction in which he expressed it, and the artificial and intellectual character which such rules stamped on poetry was heightened by the high value put on *zae*, 'wit'. Chroniclers and lawgivers still worked in Chinese as a medium and courtiers found it did their reputation no harm to be known for their ability to turn a Chinese verse: as a result, Japanese poetry was often resorted to in a mood of frivolous relaxation, for this frequently flippant society was not slow to seize the chance to go playful and carefree. But the game sometimes turned sour and brought sadness, as in this passage in *Ise Monogatari* (p. 72):

In the marsh, iris flowers were blooming prettily. One of the group, on seeing the flowers, said, 'Would you make a travel poem, each line beginning with the syllables of the name of this flower?' So he recited:

> I In the capital is the one I love, like
> R Robes of stuff so precious, yet now threadbare.
> I I have come far on this journey,
> S Sad and tearful are my thoughts.

All were moved by this same sadness and wept, their tears falling on the dried rice and making it sodden.

The poetic monument of the first half of the Heian period is *Kokinshū* (*Collection of Poems Ancient and Modern*), which comprised over 1,100 *tanka*. Its principal compiler, Ki Tsurayuki, in his famous *Preface*, also formulated Japan's poetic, in such firm terms that there has since been little divergence. The time was ripe for such a statement, for the literary consciousness that was part of the spirit of the age had been enhanced by the growing popularity of the poetry contest in which court poets competed publicly on prescribed topics, their poems and performance and the judges' verdicts giving rise to much literary discussion and disputation.

Tsurayuki begins his *Preface* with a statement of the essence and origins of Japanese poetry:

Poetry has its seeds in man's heart ... Man's activities are various and whatever he sees or hears touches his heart and is expressed in poetry. When we hear the voice of the nightingale among the blossoms, when we hear the frog in the water, we know that every living being is capable of song. Poetry, without effort, can move heaven and earth, can touch the gods and spirits ... it turns the hearts of man and woman to each other and it soothes the soul of the fierce warrior.

Japanese poetry, then, is concerned with the heart, with the heart's response to the impressions of the eye and ear. We are thus channelled into the emotions, the realm of feeling, the lyrical; there is little opportunity or desire to escape to the intellect or the didactic.

The *Preface* goes on to state the circumstances which stimulate the poet:

... when, on a spring morning, he sees the scattered blossoms; when, on an autumn evening, he hears the falling leaves ... when he sees the dew on the grass and the foam on the water, expressions of his own brief life.

These circumstances are all pathetic and touching, and the mood of the response is almost always tinged with a sense of regret, acceptance and melancholy. Here is *aware* – one of the taste-words of the age – the sadness, the fleeting beauty in life and nature (*lacrimae rerum*, perhaps) and the melancholy in the emotional response evoked by this sadness in things.

Here too is the preoccupation with time and the passive acceptance of change which had appeared in Manyō period poetry. This spirit infuses many poems of the period (p. 67):

> Can it be that the moon has changed?
> Can it be that the spring
> Is not the spring of old times?
> Is it my body alone
> That is just the same?

and, by an anonymous poet in *Kokinshū* (p. 76):

> In this world is there
> One thing constant?
> Yesterday's depths
> In Asuka River
> Today are but shallows.

We look in vain, not only for the lively vigour of the earlier period, but again for a change of mood to the uncontrollable indignation, the exultant joy in beauty, the ethical zeal, or the intellectual searching that have fired poets in other cultures.

The latter part of the Heian period saw the breakdown of the manorial system, the fall of the Fujiwara house, rivalry between court nobles and the newly rising military class, and finally in the twelfth century the growth of a feudal society based on the authority of this military class. At the end of the twelfth century, the Shōgunate, a system of government by military leaders, was established at Kamakura, far away to the east from the old Heian capital. Civil war and social confusion left their mark on literature and the arts generally, and war tales such as *Heike Monogatari* (*The Tale of the Heike*, p. 86f.) took the place of the diaries of court ladies. New branches of Buddhism, such as Zen, the soldiers' sect, and the popular Amidist faiths, came to challenge the hold of the more aristocratic Shingon and Tendai doctrines of earlier Heian times. Buddhist terms invaded everyday language and there were few literary forms that did not show the influence of Buddhism.

The intensity and the gloomy solitude of the literature of the period are eloquently expressed in the opening phrases of *Hōjōki* (*A Record of My Hut*), by Kamo Chōmei (d. 1216), a one-time court poet who became a Buddhist priest:

The river flows on and on, yet its water is never the same. The froth that sits on the backwaters vanishes and is born again but does not live for long. So also, the world over, are men and their houses. Among the stately buildings of the capital, ranging roof on roof, vying tile with tile, the houses of the high or the humble may seem to outlive generation after generation, never to fall in ruins. Yet they are few, the houses that have stood long. Either they burnt down a year ago and were rebuilt only this year, or vast mansions have toppled to become meagre huts.

This passage is full of the *sabi*, loneliness, and *yūgen*, mysterious depth, that were the aesthetic bywords of the day.

Yet the *tanka* continued to flourish under court patronage, principally because, although the court had lost its place in government, it still retained its leadership in matters of culture. The soldiers of the administration, rather than create their own, adopted the cultural fashions of the court. The court artists, deprived of their functions in government, were driven in on their art, made it their life and approached it in earnest. Fujiwara Shunzei (1114–1204) is said to have prepared himself for poetic composition by winding himself into a taut, tense, almost ritualistic mood, and his son Teika (1162–1241) would put on formal robes and cap, smooth out all creases in his clothes and sit stiffly facing south to write. As a result, in *Shinkokin-shū* (*New Collection of Poems Ancient and Modern*), the eighth Imperial anthology, ordered by Emperor Gotoba in 1201, the poetry, like the approach of the poets, was earnest and formal. Critical senses became ever more sharp and disputes between rival poets developed into wrangles between schools, between the conservatives (at first the Fujiwara house, such as Michitoshi (1047–99) and Mototoshi (1056–1142) and then the Rokujō branch within the Fujiwara house) and the innovators who strove to incorporate new freedoms in matters of both treatment and diction. The innovators were represented by the Minamoto house, Tsunenobu (1016–97) and Shunrai (1057–1129) and then by the Nijō branch of the Fujiwaras, led by Shunzei and Teika (pp. xvii, xviii).

It is natural that one of the symptoms of this and the following age should be a neo-classical nostalgia, on the part of court circles at least, for the good old Heian days. After the fall of the Shōgunate at Kamakura, a short period during which the Emperor regained authority led to a new shōgunal regime which set up its headquarters in Kyōto (the site, Muromachi, gave its name to the age) and controlled Japan until the latter part of the sixteenth century. These were years of dissension and destruction, and literary products were stagnant. The arts became status symbols for jacked-up sergeant-majors who rubbed shoulders in the Kyōto streets with the descendants of the exquisitely tasteful Heian nobility and soon found that these same descendants were ready to impart their heritage – to pupils who discovered that the past and its arts were easier to study. Through all the disturbance and disorder, the church stayed strong enough to shelter the arts, leaving its imprint increasingly deeply.

The life and writings of Yoshida Kenkō (1283–1350) are typical of all these trends. Born into a Shintō priestly family with a long tradition of high office, and as a young man a *samurai* and a poet of some repute, he retired from the world and lived as a Buddhist recluse in the hills above Kyōto, where he wrote his *Tsure-zure-gusa* (*The Grass of Idleness*), a collection of occasional jottings. He found much that was unattractive in the extremes of profusion and bad taste occasioned by the aping and class-jumping of soldiers turned courtiers:

I should call it the mark of vulgarity to have all manner of gadgets within easy reach of your seat; to have a forest of brushes alongside your inkstone; to have a row of Buddhist images ranged in your home altar; to have a profusion of stones and plants in your garden; to have hordes of children and children's children tumbling about your house; to overwhelm everyone you meet with a torrent of words and to write out at length a weary list of your good works for recitation before the Buddha. But I should not find it unbecoming if your shelves were stacked with books or your dustbin piled high with rubbish.

In this age, poetic talents were directed principally to the composition of *renga*, a series of linked verses, which were soon hedged by an elaborate list of rules and often seem to be more a social than a literary phenomenon, and of *utai*, the lyrics of the *Nō* drama.

In the chaotic final century of the Muromachi period – the Age of Kingdoms at War, to give it its Japanese title – military leaders established themselves in local strongholds and struggled with each other for supremacy. Peace did not come until 1615, with the defeat of the last forces holding out against Tokugawa Ieyasu, who had been appointed Shōgun in 1603 with headquarters in Edo, now Tokyo, and established a regime that was to rule Japan until 1868.

The last years of the previous age had heralded the social and literary developments of the Edo period. Art and culture were lavish and luxurious almost to the point of vulgarity, reflecting the decline in authority both of the urbane and elegant taste of the courtly influence of Kyōto and of the austere severity of the military and Zen. The most significant development of these years was the spread and growth of wealth and the extension of learning beyond the confines of the capital. New commercial centres like Sakai and Ōsaka grew unhindered, in large measure, by military or bureaucratic meddling, and the *chōnin*, the bourgeoisie of such thriving cities, came to wield great influence, in spite of, and in part because of, never gaining recognition from the regime; the *chōnin* were placed at the bottom of the official social ladder – even lower than farmers – and were not liable for the obligations to the state incurred by those ranked higher than they. The spirit of Edo literature is that of these *chōnin* who were its main creators and who moulded it to suit their own tastes and reflect their own activities. The novels of Saikaku and the *kabuki* theatre portrayed the *chōnin's* world, and the new poetry gathered its images from daily life; *ukiyoe* (genre) painters drew *chōnin* scenes, and the cheeky twang of the newly introduced *samisen* replaced the more genteel tones of the *koto* as the favourite instrument for accompaniment.

The *tanka* survived – indeed, a new group of 'national scholars' studied the ancient literature, and there was a revival of Chinese classical learning. But the robust vitality and the humour of this new social class was diverted into the new forms of *haiku* and *jōruri*, the dramatic ballad which was the basis of the puppet theatre, and *kabuki*, the drama of the city bourgeoisie, just as the *Nō* had been that of the previous regime. Participation in the arts enabled the new class at once to boost its ego, bruised by lack of official recognition, and to secure an outlet for its untaxed wealth.

There are two main periods in the history of Edo literature, the dividing line occurring early in the eighteenth century. In the first part, the newly vital *chōnin* class was securing freedom from many of the artificial restraints that had existed since Kamakura times, and the centre of these activities was, for the most part, in the west, in Kyōto and Ōsaka. In the second half, the centre moved east to Edo and, apart from a revival in the Temmei period, the 1780s, the arts were devitalized, literature descending often to the level of mere pastime (as in *kyōka*, 'mad *tanka*', p. 131).

The origin of *haiku*, the representative poetry of the Edo period, was the linked verse of the fourteenth century, governed by all the ideals (such as *yūgen*) and all the conventions of the *tanka*. This could not be entirely satisfying to the *chōnin*, with their demands for freedom of expression, form and subject and, in the closing years of the Muromachi period, these came to find an outlet in *haikai*, light or humorous linked verse. *Haiku* is the three-line form (five, seven and five syllables) detached from and independent of the series, yet complete in itself.

Satire and jest are the tone of the poems of Moritake (p. 101) and Sōkan (p. 102) the originators of *haikai*; then, early in the Edo period, the school of Teitoku (p. 105) attempted to return to the spirit of *renga* but only succeeded in creating a dull monotone, hedged around with complicated rules. The *Danrin* school, founded by Sōin (1605–82), reacted against this trend but went too far in the direction of excessive wit and frivolity, and it was left to Bashō (pp. 105–7), a former member of the *Danrin* school, to formulate the direction *haiku* and *tanka* were to take.

Although the avowed aim of the innovators was to create a form free of all the shackles of *tanka*, Bashō took pains to ensure that *haiku* avoided plain vulgarity; poetry was to be brought back to daily life, was to use the language and imagery (sparrows for nightingales; snails for blossom) so long tabooed by the *tanka*, but such realism need not entail vulgarity. The poet should 'mingle with the herd yet preserve a noble mind'; he should 'beautify plain speech'; he should always retain his sympathy with frailty, and feel for the *sabi* – patinated loneliness and desolation – in nature; and, above all, he should so express the nature of the particular as to define, through it, the essence of all creation; his seventeen syllables should capture a vision into the nature of the world.

The Japanese language assists the *haiku* poet's intuitive leap from the particular to the universal. Verbs are not committed to time or tense, person or number. Freed from the constraints of everyday relationships, the *haiku* poet can escape to his seventeen-syllable limbo in the world of the universal, untrammelled by the commitments of the everyday.

The intuitive flash of Zen Buddhism affects the structures of the best *haiku*, among them Bashō's most famous poem.

Furu ike ya	Old pond
Kawazu tobikomu	Frog jumps in
Mizu no oto	Sound of water

The structure is, first, the unchanging, then the momentary, and, finally, the splash, the point of intersection of the two.

The different moods of the three lines are reinforced by the pattern of vowels and consonants which Bashō uses. The mood of the still, misty pond in the first line is reinforced by the repetition of *u u* in *furu*. In the middle line, the stark suddenness of the action is underlined by the alliterative repetition of *k k* and the assonance of *a a*. The initial mood of still calm returns at the end of the final line with the assonance of *o o o*.

Buson (p. 113), the creator of the Temmei style, was more of an escapist; he preferred grandeur to Bashō's serenity and sensuous colour to Bashō's subjective symbolism.

Issa (pp. 115–17) brought *haiku* down to the level of the common man. His diction was much more that of the street, and his personal miseries awakened in him a deep compassion for other living beings which he uses to satirize man's heartlessness (p. 117):

> For fleas, also, the night
> Must be so very long,
> So very lonely.

After the many restraints put on *tanka*, *haiku* might appear as something of a free-for-all. But there were restrictions, for example, on diction where excessive use of the colloquial would bring frowns; the seventeen syllables should ideally – and nearly always did – end in a noun or an emotional ejaculation and should contain their 'season word' (*kigo*) or expression hinting at the time of the year appropriate to the context. Thus, Bashō's frog is a spring theme and Issa's fleas set the season in summer.

Many *kigo* are self-explanatory: thus, for spring, cherry blossoms (*hana*) or spring rain (*harusame*); cicada (*semi*) or evening shower (*yūdachi*) for summer; autumn evening (*aki no kure*) or the harvest moon (*meigetsu*) for autumn; and winter seclusion (*fuyugomori*) or cold winter shower (*shigure*) for winter. Others are less obvious; the western ear needs time even to become indifferent to, much less sympathetic towards, the croaks of the bullfrog, and the association of this sound with the burgeoning of spring is neither natural nor automatic. Again, only a sensibility in close accord with that of the Japanese would at once make the transition from the insistent beat of the fulling block to the chill stillness of autumn's night, while the mention of the scarecrow does not immediately evoke scenes of bare and deserted fields in late autumn after the harvest.

Another seventeen-syllable form, *senryū* (p. 124f), developed in the latter half of the Edo period. Like *haiku*, it was unrestricted in subject and style, but it was less severely controlled in the matter of the use of the colloquial language; it dispensed with the season word of *haiku* and ended usually with a verb in place of the latter's noun or emotive ejaculation. There were also differences of tone and elevation. *Senryū* contains none of the mysticism of Bashō's *haiku*; it stops short at the particular and deals in distortions and failings, not in the beauty of nature (p. 127):

> 'She may have only one eye
> But it's a pretty one,'
> Says the go-between.

4. *The Modern Period*

Tanka and Haiku

It was with the two traditional forms, *tanka* and *haiku*, that Japan faced the world after more than two centuries of seclusion enforced by the Tokugawa Shōgunate. Although the 'modern' period begins with the Meiji Restoration in 1868, it was not until the late 1880s or 1890s that the new atmosphere began to affect Japanese literary movements. But once the impact both of a foreign stimulus and an indigenous revival was felt, their effect became ever more extensive.

The trends of mainstream development in both *tanka* and *haiku* styles were set primarily by Shiki (pp. 151, 156). Shiki's contribution was part of the general literary renaissance of the middle years of the Meiji period (1868–1912). Shiki's purpose was to preserve the natural: 'Be natural,' he advises *haiku* composers, 'prefer real pictures.' It was this objectivity that made him single out Buson rather than Bashō and that also recommended the straightforward and direct style of *Manyōshū*, rather than *Kokinshū*, to the *Araragi* (*Yew*) school of *tanka* that was founded in 1908 by his followers under Itō Sachio (p. 150) and Saitō Mokichi (p. 152). In the meanwhile, the early years of this century proved a prosperous period for the *Myōjō* (*Morning Star*) school, its romanticism affecting poets such as Yosano Akiko (p. 151), Ishikawa Takuboku (p. 153), Kitahara Hakushū, and Takamura Kōtarō. The closing years of the Meiji period were marked by a general swing from realism to naturalism and Wakayama Bokusui's (p. 155) move away from high lyricism was part of the spirit of the times. However, the mainstream *Araragi* realists regained a position of ascendancy which they held until the end of the Pacific War.

Shiki's dictum, 'prefer real pictures', became the foundation of the objectivism of the *haiku* journal *Hototogisu* (*Cuckoo*) which, with Kyoshi, he founded in 1898 and which remained the most influential *haiku* publication in Japan. Early disciples were Hekigotō (p. 158) and Meisetsu (p. 156), but soon Hekigotō, at the head of an anti-classical and anti-traditionalist faction (creating a free *haiku* which did not acknowledge a syllable count), broke away from the mainstream group led by Kyoshi (p. 158) and supported by Suiha (p. 159), Dakotsu (p. 160) and Sekitei (p. 160).

The Taishō period (1912–26) was marked by a revival of interest in Bashō, as a result of which subjective tendencies appeared, assisted by the wide study of Europe's symbolists. In the Shōwa period (from 1926) Kyoshi was joined in the *Hototogisu* mainstream school by Shūōshi (p. 161), Bōsha (p. 162), Kusadao (p. 163), and Takashi (p. 164). Hakyō (p. 164) and Shūson (p. 163) are representative of the 'new-style *haiku*' group which campaigned against the objective imagery of the *Hototogisu* school.

Shintaishi ('New-Style Poetry')

The origin of 'new-style poetry' is usually traced to the publication in July 1882 (by a historian, a professor of Oriental thought and a botanist) of a volume of translations of, among others, Bloomfield, Longfellow, Tennyson, Gray's *Elegy*, excerpts from *Henry IV* Part 2 and *Hamlet*, together with experimental poems by the compilers, which included such titles as 'The principles of sociology' and 'On making a pilgrimage to the Great Buddha at Kamakura'.

This collection was followed seven years later by *Omokage* (*Semblances*) from a publishing house called New Voices. Many of the translations were the work of Mori Ōgai, at one time Surgeon-General in the Imperial Army and one of the leading novelists of the day. *Semblances* included translations of Byron, Goethe, Heine, Shakespeare and a number of Chinese originals.

However, neither translations nor original 'new-style poems' had as yet succeeded in going outside the traditional five-seven form and the 'new-style poets' were still writing, in effect, the *chōka* of the Manyō period or the Heian *imayō* style. Ophelia's song offered Mori Ōgai a perfect prototype:

How should I your true-love know	*Izure wo kimi ga / koibito to*
From another one?	*Wakite shirubeki / sube ya aru*
By his cockle hat and staff,	*Kai no kammuri to / tsuku-zue to*
And his sandal shoon . . .	*Hakeru kutsu to zo / shirushi naru*
He is dead and gone, lady,	*Kare wa shinikeri / waga hime yo*
He is dead and gone;	*Kare wa yomiji e / tachinikeri*
At his head a grass-green turf,	*Kashira no kata no / koke wo miyo*
At his heels a stone . . .	*Ashi no kata ni wa / ishi tateri*
White his shroud as the mountain snow . . .	*Hitsugi wo ōu / kinu no iro wa*
Larded with sweet flowers;	*Takane no yuki to / mimagainu*
Which bewept to the grave did go,	*Namida yadoseru / hana no wa wa*
With true-love showers.	*Nuretaru mama ni / hōmurinu*

'New-Style Poetry' to 1945

The earliest 'new-style poems' in our selection are traditional in form. Tōson's *Song of travel on the Chikuma River* (p. 170) begins

> Kinō mata / kakute arikeri
> Kyō mo mata / kakute arinamu

and the whole is of twelve-syllable lines, with a caesura after the fifth syllable and four lines to a stanza. Bansui's *Moon over the ruined castle* (p. 169) is of similar form, the caesura in the twelve-syllable line here occurring after the seventh. The same is true of diction, for the colloquial style did not succeed the literary until the beginning of this century. Takamura Kōtarō (p. 172) and Hagiwara Sakutarō (p. 177) were among the pioneers in the use of 'new-style' diction in 'new-style' poetry. However, once the new import of free verse had taken root, it was adopted with a wholehearted zeal quite characteristic of this culture that has always been so ready to incorporate from outside. But the freedom of form and the liberal adoption of the colloquial idiom did leave 'modern poetry' open to the charge, often levelled by traditionalists and often appropriate, that it does not 'fight' (i.e. contrast) sufficiently with prose.

A prominent feature of the story of the development of *shintaishi* ('new-style poetry') is the growth of schools or coteries which reproduced nearly every trend of European fashion. There were rapid and sometimes bewildering switches by individual poets from one school to another. Thus, Takuboku, earlier an ultra-romanticist – and still known as such in Japan – could write in 1911, the year before his death, a 'socialist' poem of the kind of *After a fruitless argument* (p. 175).

In the 1880s and 1890s Japanese romantics were the leading group, centred on the journal *Bungakkai* (*Literary World*), one of whose co-founders in 1894 was Shimazaki Tōson (p. 169).

At the end of the nineteenth century and early in the twentieth, both romanticism and naturalism claimed many adherents among *shintaishi* poets. The romantics grouped in the New Poetry Society and wrote for its journal *Myōjō* (*Bright Star*). Leading members of this coterie included Takamura Kōtarō (p. 172), Kitahara Hakushū (p. 174) and Ishikawa Takuboku (p. 175).

Japan's first symbolists came on the scene in the first decade of the twentieth century. Kambara Ariake (p. 171) was an early leader of this group. Then, towards the end of the decade, the establishment of the Pan Society offered a focus around which the romantics were able to regroup.

During the Taishō period (1912–26) the movement for 'new-style poetry' in the colloquial language, begun in the 1880s, finally reached full expression through the contributions especially of Hagiwara Sakutarō (p. 177) and Murō Saisei, both members of the *Kanjō (Feelings)* group.

The 1920s saw a rash of Surrealism, Cubism, Futurism and Dadaism – Takahashi Shinkichi (p. 196) issued his *Dadaist Manifesto* in 1922 and in the following year published a collection *Poems of the Dadaist Shinkichi*. Many new poetry journals appeared, some of them given the epithet '*sangōrashii*' – 'looking likely to fold after volume three'!

The Japan Socialist League was established in 1920 and proletarian poets published in *Aka to Kuro (Red and Black)*, founded by Tsuboi Shigeji (p. 180) and Okamoto Jun (p. 198) in 1923. They were joined later by Nakano Shigeharu (p. 204), one of the foremost Proletarian poets.

The journal *Shi to Shiron (Poetry and Poetics)*, founded in 1928, soon became the focus of a group which valued theory and 'pure poetry' and attracted intellectuals and modernists sympathetic to the ideas of its co-founders Nishiwaki Junzaburō (p. 189) and Miyoshi Tatsuji (p. 195).

Another group which gathered around Kusano Shimpei (p. 207) in the 1920s eventually in 1935 became the *Rekitei (Course of History)* coterie. Prominent members were the realists Kaneko Mitsuharu (p. 190) and Miyazawa Kenji (p. 193) and the group also included Yagi Jūkichi (p. 194), Hara Tamiki (p. 211) and Nakahara Chūya (p. 212).

A seminal event in the development of *shintaishi* was the publication of the journal *Shiki (Four Seasons)* in 1933. *Shiki* poets were lyricists, led in the first place by co-editors Miyoshi Tatsuji (p. 155) and Maruyama Kaoru (p. 194). Prominent *Shiki* group members included co-founder Hagiwara Sakutarō (p. 177), Horiguchi Daigaku (p. 184), Satō Haruo

(p. 186), Tanaka Fuyuji (p. 187), Takenaka Iku (p. 209) and the younger Tachihara Michizō (p. 214) and Kinoshita Yūji (p. 216).

'New-Style Poetry' from 1945

The Pacific War silenced many of Japan's leading *shintaishi* poets, and the shock of defeat in 1945 apparently stunned Japan's poets more than most of her artists. The first poets to emerge in the bleak early post-war months belonged to the Proletarian literature group, some of whose members had suffered internment.

One of the earliest new groups to appear after the end of the Pacific War was *Arechi* (*Waste Land*), taking its name from T. S. Eliot's poem, which had been translated into Japanese by Nishiwaki Junzaburō. The name of the school matched the desolate and gloomy waste that was Japan in the first years of the peace. Prominent among *Arechi* poets were Kuroda Saburō (p. 216), Tamura Ryūichi (p. 220), who both moved later to the *Rekitei* group, and Nakae Toshio (p. 243). Tamura's writing in the early post-war period expresses more vividly than any other the violent and destructive character of Japanese poetry of the second half of the 1940s.

From about the end of 1952, Japan began to pull out of the abject poverty and deprivation of the immediate post-war years and to reappraise Japanese values abandoned all too hastily in the immediate post-war swing to Western ideals. By 1956 there had evolved a synthesis with which most were able to identify. The Japanese said of themselves at the time that they had 'calmed down' (*ochitsuita*).

These changes are reflected in the poetry of the time. In 1952, with the publication of his collection entitled *The Isolation of Two Billion Light Years* (p. 238), Tanikawa Shuntarō was hailed as the first poet of the post-war generation. In the following year, 1953, Tanikawa founded the *Kai* (*Oar*) group with Yoshino Hiroshi (p. 225), Ibaragi Noriko (p. 227), Iijima Kōichi (p. 229), Kawasaki Hiroshi (p. 230), Ōoka Makoto (p. 231) and Nakae Toshio (p. 243).

Members of the *Kai* school were lyric poets. Representative of their stance was the fresh lyricism of Tanikawa's early poems, expressing the new hopes of the Japanese at the time and offering an alternative to the nihilism of the *Arechi* poets. Tanikawa is one of the most widely known figures of the post-war Japanese literary scene, through the range of his activities in radio, film and television and the breadth of his writing – picture books, children's stories, drama and song lyrics as well as poetry.

The first six months of 1960 saw almost nightly demonstrations in Tokyo against the renewal of the Security Treaty between Japan and the US. Japan's intellectuals and artists emerged from this unrest with a new confidence bolstered by the economic well-being which followed from the official income-doubling policy of the first half of the 1960s. The Tokyo Olympics of 1964, a distinct pre-satellite success, enabled Japan to show herself off to the world: Japan joined the comity of the world's sporting nations and in so doing purged herself of any vestigial feelings of wartime guilt.

During these years – the early 1960s – the *Wani* (*Crocodile*) group of surrealists came into being. Co-founders were Yoshioka Minoru (p. 217), the leading post-war surrealist poet, Iijima Kōichi (p. 229) and Ōoka Makoto (p. 231). Ōoka, one of the most respected and prolific historians of classical and modern Japanese poetry, continues to exercise a very great influence on the contemporary literary scene.

From the 1960s, *shintaishi* poets broadened their interests beyond the narrow limits of poetry alone to working in radio, television and the theatre. Writing for children – poetry and stories – is a regular aspect of *shintaishi* poets' work and many have published collections of criticism and influential translations.

Public readings have become a favourite activity among Japanese poets, many of whom are prepared to travel the world to take part in readings or to hear their poems (and translations of them) performed. Some *shintaishi* poets have developed their own distinctive reading techniques: 'like a trance-song' is one description of the performances of Yoshimasu Gōzō (p. 246).

The number of women *shintaishi* poets has grown rapidly since the 1960s and 1970s. The best known is Shiraishi Kazuko (p. 234). Born in Vancouver in 1931, she has maintained a high level of literary activity in essays, criticism and translation since her first collection was published in the early 1950s. For the past twenty-five years she has been especially conspicuous as a performance poet.

Also prominent among contemporary women *shintaishi* poets are Isaka Yōko (p. 247) and Itō Hiromi (p. 253). They share a concern with words and both are seeking to create distinctive new forms of language. Itō Hiromi plays with words in *Glenn Gould Goldberg* (p. 255) and *Bad Breasts* (p. 253), with its reference to Melanie Klein, expresses her interest in the female body and feminist poetics.

Feminine concern with language is a variation on one of the most general themes of contemporary *shintaishi* poets, who share these attempts to create new forms of language with poets of many other cultures, and particularly the San Francisco and the New York schools. Poets play with sounds and with words, seeking to invent new ones by, for example, substituting consonants or vowels in regular patterns. Such games are facilitated by the simplicity of the consonant-vowel Japanese syllabary (see pp. lxvii f.) and aided by the ubiquitous *wāpuro* (word processor). There are examples in the work of Tanikawa Shuntarō (p. 239) and Itō Hiromi (p. 255). The title of a poem by Ōoka Makoto, *Words Words* (p. 232), speaks for itself, and Asabuki Ryōji's *96 I classify* (p. 249), a prose poem, is a light-hearted classification of a long list of words.

If sheer volume is any indication, contemporary *shintaishi* poetry is alive and well. Two publishing houses produce collections by individual poets, and a recent anthology of *shintaishi* poetry from the nineteenth century to the present day selects from the works of over 200 poets and runs to 611 pages. Two of the compilers are Ōoka Makoto and Tanikawa Shuntarō, both born in 1931, who include the work of nearly forty poets younger than themselves.

I reproduce the 1963 statement of my thanks in the introduction to the first edition of the *Penguin Book of Japanese Verse.*

I am indebted to a great number of colleagues and friends: I hope that they will not think my gratitude any the less sincere if they do not find themselves in the list of those whom it would be churlish not to mention by name.

First I must thank the many poets and their publishers who so readily gave permission for our translations; Professor Hiramatsu,

Professor Nishiwaki, Kusano Shimpei, and Fukuda Rikutarō, who all gladly offered valued and expert advice; Mr Hanyūda, who helped with the choice of poems in the earlier periods; Mr W. McAlpine, formerly of the British Council in Tokyo, who generously drew on his wide range of literary friendships; Mr Yamashida and Mr Mutō, of the Japanese National Commission for UNESCO, who offered valuable facilities in Japan; Professor N. Saigō and Mr S. Miyamoto of the School of Oriental and African Studies, University of London; Mr N. Hagihara, formerly of St Antony's College, Oxford and Mr K. Miyakawa of the Embassy of Japan in London; Brian Powell and Ann Draycon for reading and advising on my translations before I passed them on to Anthony Thwaite; and Delia Twamley for typing and tidying up the manuscript so efficiently.

Geoffrey Bownas
Oxford
October 1963

During the intervening years and recently, in preparing this new edition, I have been helped by a large number of colleagues and friends, both English and Japanese. Again, they are too numerous to allow all to be named. I hope that those whose names are not recorded will accept this general 'thank you'.

I would like to express my thanks to the poets and their publishers who gave permissions for our translations.

Ueno Takashi introduced me in 1979 to the daughter of Takahama Kyoshi, who is head of the *Tamamokai* group of *haiku* poets. Friend-ships with *Tamamokai* have stayed warm and my translation (p. 159) of Kyoshi's poem written in Kew Gardens in 1936 is placed alongside the original Japanese poem in the Japanese Garden in Kew.

My work with Mishima Yukio during his last summer in 1970 on *New Writing in Japan*, published by Penguin Books in 1972, also created a number of associations which have lasted, particularly with Shiraishi Kazuko and Takahashi Mutsuo. I still find Japan without Mishima poorer and lonelier.

More recently I have received tremendous help and have benefited greatly from the infectious enthusiasm for this new edition of Mike Sharrocks, Librarian of Gyosei International College in Reading. His assistants, Naoko Furuichi and Chiyoko Burch, have been tireless in seeking out collections of the work of contemporary poets.

Sakurai Tomoyuki, Director until July 1997 of the Japan Foundation London Office, has been truly generous with his support.

Among the poets themselves, in addition to Shiraishi Kazuko and Takahashi Mutsuo, I have had invaluable help from Tanikawa Shuntarō who offered a list of *shintaishi* poets from the nineteenth century to the present who should be included and presented us with a copy of his anthology as soon as it was published, late in 1996. I have used it unsparingly as a guide to what the Japanese judge to be the best and most typical poets and the best parts of their work.

Finally, I have been helped in the preparation of the manuscript of this new edition by Wiesia Cook, who has given unstinting and highly efficient support and to whom I dedicate the new translations in this edition.

Geoffrey Bownas
London
September 1998

Chronological Tables

Nara	AD 710—94
Heian	794—1185
Kamakura	1185—1338
Muromachi	1338—1603
Edo	1603—1868
Meiji	1868—1912
Taishō	1912—26
Shōwa	1926—89
Heisei	1989—

Table of Dates

660 BC   Emperor Jimmu completes the conquest of Yamato (according to tradition)

AD

Fifth century   Adoption of Chinese script

552   Introduction of Buddhism

646   Taika administrative reforms

710   Nara becomes first permanent capital

712   Compilation of *Kojiki*, first official chronicle

720   Compilation of *Nihon Shoki*, official chronicle

752   Dedication of the Great Buddha at Nara

794   Transfer of capital to Heian-kyō (Kyōto)

Ninth century.   Rise of Fujiwara house

c. 905   Compilation of *Kokinshū*, first Imperial anthology

c. 940   Start of rise of Taira house

Eleventh century (late).   Decline of Fujiwara house

1156   Hōgen civil war. Start of dominance of Taira house

1159   Heiji civil war

1185   Taira house overthrown by Minamoto house

1192   Kamakura Shōgunate founded by Minamoto Yoritomo

1205   Start of Regency of Hōjō house

1274–81   Unsuccessful invasion attempts by Mongols

1333   Kamakura Shōgunate overthrown

1338   Muromachi Shōgunate set up in Kyōto by Ashikaga Takauji

Fifteenth century.   Civil war and disturbances

1467   Ōnin civil war, collapse of government

Sixteenth century.   All Japan involved in civil war

1542   Arrival of Portuguese in Japan

1549   Arrival of St Francis Xavier

1568   Oda Nobunaga becomes Shōgun

1582   Toyotomi Hideyoshi succeeds Nobunaga

1592
1597 } Unsuccessful expeditions against Korea

1603   Tokugawa Ieyasu becomes first Tokugawa Shōgun

1615   Siege of Ōsaka; Ieyasu supreme

1639   Japan closed to foreigners

1688–1703   Genroku era, flowering of *chōnin* culture

1853   Perry arrives in Japan

1867   End of Tokugawa Shōgunate

1868   Meiji Restoration; feudalism gives way to monarchy

1894   Start of Sino-Japanese War

1904   Start of Russo-Japanese War

1932   Manchurian Incident

1937   China Incident

1941   Japan enters World War II

1945   Japan defeated and occupied by Allied Powers

1951   San Francisco Peace Treaty: first US Japan Security Treaty

1952   Japan regains independence with end of Occupation

1953   Television broadcasting begins

1955   First transistor radios on sale

1956   White Paper on the Economy marks the 'end of the post-war period'
        Japan joins UN

1960   Demonstrations against second US–Japan Security Treaty

1964   High-speed Shinkansen train network opens
        18th Summer Olympic Games in Tokyo (the first Asian venue)

Primitive Poetry and the Nara Period

(to AD 794)

Song of proposal

This crab — where does it come from?
From Tsuruga, a hundred towns away.
Creeping sideways, how far did it crawl?
It hurried to Ichiji Isle, to the Isle of Beauty.[1]

The dabchick plunges,
Breathless and gulping:
I plunged hurriedly
Up and down the slopes
Of the Sasanami Way.
The maiden I met with
On the Kohata Road —
Seen from behind,
Slender as a shield:
The rows of her teeth
Like tiny acorns.

The earth of Wani Slope at Ichii,
The topsoil red as flesh,
The earth underneath
Black, black as jet:
She took the middle earth,
Like the middle of three chestnuts,
And keeping it from the sun
That blinds, makes you bend your head,
She marked her eyebrows in,
Painting them thick, deep-arched.

The girl I saw
And wanted this way,
The girl I saw
And wanted that way,

Is here at the banquet,
Sitting before my eyes,
Sitting at my side.

Come, then, my men,
To pluck wild garlic,
To pluck wild garlic,
And, on our road,
The fragrant-scented
Orange tree in flower,
Its topmost twigs
Withered by perching birds,
Its lowest branches
Snapped and killed by men.
But the middle branches,
Like the chestnut's kernel,
Where the reddening fruit nestles –
Oh! the ripening maiden! –
If we tempted her on,
She would be so good!

PRINCE KINASHI NO KARU

We built mountain paddies
On the broad-flanked hills,
And the hills were so tall
We led water conduits through the ground.
The sister whom I won
With a secret victory,[2]
Secret as those conduits –
The wife for whom I wept
With a hidden grief –
This day, indeed, we lie,
Our skins grafting.

On the bamboo-grass
The hail beats and rattles.
But when, unbeaten,
I have slept sound,
Let them plot and plan:
When we two have slept,
I and my beloved,
Let there be tangle and chaos
Like the tangle when reeds are cut –
When we two have slept.

The Palace of Hishiro at Makimuku
Basks in the daytime sun,
Flashes in the evening sun,
Its roots firm as the bamboo,
Stretching like a tree:
A palace weighed down
With eight hundred earth-loads.
The flourishing zelkova
That stands by the Hall
Of the First Tasting at the Gate of Cypress –
Its topmost branches
Screen the sky;
Its middle branches
Screen my lady;
Its lower branches
Screen my land.
A leaf from the tip
Of the topmost branch
Settles on the middle branch;
A leaf from the tip
Of the middle branch
Settles on the lower branch;
A leaf from the tip
Of the lower branch
Settles on the oil
Floating in the flashing jade goblet

Offered by the maiden of Mie,
Mie of the bright silk.
The water churns and curdles.
How majestic, how joyous,
August Child of the Sun high-shining.

EMPRESS IWA NO HIME

Longing for the Emperor

My Lord has departed
And the time has grown long.
Shall I search the mountains,
Going forth to meet you,
Or wait for you here?

No! I would not live,
Longing for you.
On the mountain crag, rather,
Rock-root as my pillow,
Dead would I lie.

Yet even if it be so
I shall wait for my Lord,
Till on my black hair —
Trailing fine in the breeze —
The dawn's frost shall fall.

In the autumn field,
Over the rice ears,
The morning mist trails,
Vanishing somewhere . . .
Can my love fade too?

EMPEROR YŪRYAKU

With her basket, her basket,
And her trowel, her trowel,
On this hill a girl picks grasses.
I would ask about her home,
Ask her to tell me her name.[3]

The land of Yamato
Is equal with the heavens.
It is I that rule it all,
It is I reign over all.
Thus I tell my home, my name.

EMPEROR JOMEI

Climbing Mount Kagu

In the land of Yamato
The mountains cluster;
But the best of all mountains
Is Kagu, dropped from heaven.
I climbed, and stood, and viewed my lands.
Over the broad earth
Smoke-mist hovers.
Over the broad water
Seagulls hover.
Beautiful, my country,
My Yamato,
Island of the dragonfly.[4]

PRINCE ARIMA

On preparing for a journey

1

On the beach of Iwashiro,
I pull and knot together
The branches of the pine.[5]
If my fate turns out well,
I shall return to see them again.

2

If I were at home,
We should pile rice in a bowl.
With grass for my pillow,
Now that I journey,
It is heaped on pasania leaves.

PRINCESS NUKADA

Poem written on the occasion of Emperor Tenji's ordering Fujiwara Kamatari to judge between the claims of spring and autumn

When the spring comes
After winter's confining,
The birds that did not sing
Come out and sing;
The flowers that were closed
Come out and bloom.
But the mountain trees grow dense –
We cannot reach to pick the flowers:
The weed-grasses are thick –
We cannot see the flowers we pick.

We see the leaves
On an autumn hill;
We pick the red leaves,
Admiring and praising;
We leave the green ones,
Sighing and grieving.
There lies my regret:
Autumn hills for me.

Three tanka

1
We wait for the moon
To put out
From Nikitatsu.
The tide swells to the full.
Come, let us row.

2
You went to fields madder-red.
You went to your royal lands.
The keeper watched
As you beckoned me
With your sleeve.

3
I waited and I
Yearned for you.
My blind
Stirred at the touch
Of the autumn breeze.

PRINCESS KAGAMI

In reply to a poem[6] by her younger sister, Princess Nukada

The wind blew: for you
It blew, a hateful wind.
I waited for this wind
To stir, to stir for me.
And now, my heart bleeds.[7]

EMPRESS SAIMEI

From the age of the gods
Man has continued,
Men in their myriads
Fill the land.
Like flights of wild duck
Bustling, they come and go.
But the one I love –
You – are not here.
All day,
Till the darkness comes,
All night,
To the lintel of the dawn,
I think of you,
Unable to sleep –
Even to the dawn
Of this long night.

Envoys

I
Over the mountain ledge
Flights of wild duck
Noisily go;

But I am lonely,
For you are not here.

2
On the Ōmi road,
From Toko Mountain
Flows Isaya, river of No Knowing.
As day piles on day,
Do you still love me?

A COURT LADY

On the death of Emperor Tenji

I am of this world,
Unfit to touch a god.
Separated from his spirit,
In the morning I grieve my Lord:
Sundered from his soul,
I long for my Lord.
Would he were jade
I might coil on my arm!
Would he were a robe
I might never put off!
I saw my Lord,
The one I love,
Last night . . . in sleep.

PRINCE ŌTSU

Poem exchanged with Lady Ishikawa

In the dew dripping
On the broad-flanked hill,

Waiting for you
I stood dampened
By the dew on the hill.

LADY ISHIKAWA

Poem exchanged with Prince Ōtsu

Waiting for me
You were dampened.
O that I could
Be the dew dripping
On that broad-flanked hill.

PRINCESS ŌKU

On Prince Ōtsu's return to Yamato after a secret visit to Ise Shrine

Sending my dear brother
Back to Yamato,
I stood in the dark of night
Till wet with dawn's dew.

Even when two go together,
The autumn mountains
Are hard to cross.
How will my Lord
Pass over them alone?

EMPRESS JITŌ

On the old lady Shii

No, no! I say
To Shii's far-fetched tales.
Still she insists.
For a time I have not heard them
And now I long for them.

OLD LADY SHII

Replying to a poem by Empress Jitō

No, no! I say,
But still you command,
'Tell on, tell on!'
So I fetch out one more –
And you say 'Far-fetched!'[8]

WORKMAN (HITOMARO?)

The construction of the Palace of Fujiwara

Our great Empress[9]
Who rules the eight quarters,
August child
Of the sun on high,
Governs her domain
And controls her palace
On the Fujiwara Plain.

At her divine desire
Gods of heaven and earth
Came and offered service.
The stout cypress logs
Of Tanakami Mount in Ōmi,
Ōmi, where waves dash the rocks,
Trailing like jewel duckweed,
We floated down the Uji waters.
Our homes forgotten,
Not thinking of ourselves,
Like a flight of wild duck
We, her servants, bobbed in the water,
Thronging to gather the beams
And carry them to the streams of Izumi.
'To the shining Palace of the Sun we build
May unknown kingdoms come in homage.'

On the Kuse Highway there appeared
That magic tortoise with the letters on his shell –
'Our land shall never fail' –
Marking a new era.
We lashed the logs as rafts
And vied to take them
Up Izumi's stream.
I look on our scurryings –
The fruit of a divinity.

PRINCESS NIU

On the death of Prince Iwata

My prince, who bent to me
Like the lithe bamboo,
My prince with sun-brown cheeks,
Is now a god among the royal tombs

Hidden in clefts of Hatsuse Hill.
So spoke the herald with the jewelled bow.
Is it rumour? Are they crooked words
That I have heard?
I did not penetrate the distant clouds,
I did not touch the meeting-point
Of heaven and earth.
This is my great sorrow,
This my great lament.
O that I had used the portent
Of the road at sunset,
The omen of the lifted stones
To build an altar in my house,
To serve my prince with wine,
With jewels and with robes,
In my hand the seven-jointed rush
Of Sasara Moor, high as heaven.
Had I but washed my stains,
Standing at the bank
Of the Divine River,
My lord would not lie
Under Hatsuse's jutting crags.

Envoys

1
Is it deceit, a lie,
That my lord is laid
On the high cliffs?

2
On Furu Hill, above
The shrine of sacred stone,[10]
The cedars cluster;
But my heart will never cede
Its yearnings for my lord.

KOKASHŪ
(*Collection of Ancient Poems*)

Through the chinks
Of the jewelled blinds
Come to me.
Should my mother ask —
Mother of the sagging breasts —
I'll say it was the wind.[11]

ANONYMOUS POEMS
from *Manyōshū*

My tangled hair
I shall not cut:
Your hand, my dearest,
Touched it as a pillow.

To meet my love
I have no way.
Like the tall peak
Of Fuji in Suruga,
Shall I burn for ever?

In the Lake of Ōmi
Are eighty harbours
And eighty islands.
On every island tip
Stands an orange-tree.
On the topmost branch
They smear birdlime.
To the middle branch
They tie a turtle-dove.
To the lowest branch

They tie a wagtail.
Their own mothers
They snare, unknowing.
Their own fathers
They snare, unknowing.
Yet they merely sport,
Turtle-dove and wagtail.[12]

The stairway up to heaven –

The stairway up to heaven –
O that it were longer!
The highest hill –
O that it were higher!
That I might bring
The night-appearing Moon God's
Draught of eternal youth[13]
And grant my love
To lose his years.

Envoy

He whom I prize
As moon and sun in heaven –
That day by day
He must grow old!

POEMS OF RIDICULE AND DERISION
from *Manyōshū*

Like the few ears salvaged
After deer and boar have plundered
Rice fields newly opened up,
My love is all shrivelled.

If my recent love-labours,
Set down in writing, were
Put forward as 'services rendered',
I'd make the Civil List (Fifth Grade).

If my recent love-labours
Do not make the grade,
I'll go lodge complaint
With the Chamberlain himself.

BEGGAR SONGS
from *Manyōshū*

The sorrows of the deer

My good sirs,
Who now sit so quiet,
Suppose you went on a journey
Unplanned, where would you be led?[14]
To the land of Kara
To capture tigers,
Bring eight heads back home,
Sew their skins as mats
And lay the mats eightfold.[15]

In the hills of Heguri,
Sloping smooth as eightfold mats,
In the fourth month and the fifth
I went on the medicine hunt.
Under two white-oak trees,
Eight catalpa bows at hand
And eight turnip-headed arrows,
I waited for the deer –
When a stag came and stood
And moaned his fate before me.
'Soon I must die.

Then I shall offer my lord
My horns as hat trimmings,
My ears as inkwells,
My eyes as clear mirrors,
My hoofs as bow-tips,
My hair as writing-brushes,
My hide as box leather,
My flesh as mincemeat,
My liver too as mincemeat,
My belly as salted flesh.
So this old servant's one body
Shall flower sevenfold,
Shall flower eightfold.
Then praise, praise me to the skies!'

The woes of the crab

In the Bay of Naniwa –
Naniwa of the flashing waves –
I huddle in the home I made.
A reed-crab, my lord commands me,
So they say, but know not the cause.
Yet I know well the circumstance.
As singer am I summoned?
As flutist am I summoned?
As harpist am I summoned?
But, obeying his commands,
When today becomes tomorrow
I come to Morrow Town:
Though downed, I reach Downham:
And while I have no stick,
I find myself on Stafford Plain.[16]
Going in the Eastern Gate
Of the castle's inner wall,
I hear my lord's commands.
Like haltered horse, I am tethered:
Like an ox, twine binds my nose.

Then from the hillside he brings
Five hundred strips of elm-tree bark,
Hangs it to dry in the shining sun,
Treads it in a Chinese mortar,
Pounds it with the garden pestle.
Thick, first-dripped salt from Naniwa Bay —
Naniwa of the flashing waves —
And swift-made potter's jars he brings.
Then he smears my eyes with salt
And says, 'A tasty dish indeed.'

AZUMA UTA

(Poems from the Eastland)

The highway to Shinano
Is but newly opened.[17]
Mind you do not trip
Over the stumps of trees.
Wear your sandals, husband.
                    [from Shinano]

The wind that sweeps down Ikaho
One day it blows, they say,
Another it does not blow.
Only my love
Knows no time.
                    [from Kamitsuke]

I pound the rice
And my hands are chapped.
Tonight, my young prince
Will take them and sigh.
                    [source unknown]

In the spring meadow
Cropping the grass,
The pony's jaw is never still.
Does she talk of me the same,
The wife I left at home?

[source unknown]

POEMS FROM NOTO

In a muddy creek
By Kumaki's waves,
He's dropped his precious axe,
He's dropped his precious axe.

He's worried, he's worried.
Stop that bloody noise:
We'll see if it will float,
We'll see if it will float.

From Table Isle
By Kashima Crag
You gathered baby cockles.
You took them home
And with a stone
You smashed their tiny shells.
In the swift stream
You washed the fish,
Rubbed them with ocean salt.
Rub-a-rub-rub.
Rub-a-rub-rub.
Put them in a tub,
Put them in a pot
And served them up on the table.
They're for your mama, eh,
Darling little girl?
They're for your papa, eh,
Darling little pet?

KAKINOMOTO HITOMARO

In praise of Empress Jitō

Our great Empress
Who rules in tranquillity,
True god of true god,
Has done a divine thing.
Deep in the valley
Of Yoshino's foaming torrents
She builds high
Her tall palace.

She climbs and looks
Across her lands:
The mountain folds,
Like green walls,
As offerings
From their deity,
When spring comes
Bring cherry garlands:
When autumn begins
They bring crimson leaves.
The river spirit too
Makes gifts of sacred food:
In the upper shoals
He sets the cormorants,
In the lower shallows
He spreads small nets.
Mountain and river too
Come near and serve
This godlike land.

Envoy

Mountain and river too
Come near and serve.
She, in her divinity,
On foaming torrents
Rides her royal craft.

I loved her like the leaves,
The lush leaves of spring
That weighed the branches of the willows
Standing on the jutting bank
Where we two walked together
While she was of this world.
My life was built on her;
But man cannot flout
The laws of this world.
To the wide fields where the heat haze shimmers,
Hidden in a white cloud,
White as white mulberry scarf,
She soared like the morning bird
Hidden from our world like the setting sun.
The child she left as token
Whimpers, begs for food; but always
Finding nothing that I might give,
Like birds that gather rice-heads in their beaks,
I pick him up and clasp him in my arms.
By the pillows where we lay,
My wife and I, as one,
The daylight I pass lonely till the dusk,
The black night I lie sighing till the dawn.
I grieve, yet know no remedy:
I pine, yet have no way to meet her.
The one I love, men say,
Is in the hills of Hagai,

So I labour my way there,
Smashing rock-roots in my path,
Yet get no joy from it.
For, as I knew her in this world,
I find not the dimmest trace.

Envoys

1

The autumn moon
We saw last year
Shines again: but she
Who was with me then
The years separate for ever.

2

On the road to Fusuma
In the Hikite Hills,
I dug my love's grave.
I trudge the mountain path
And think: 'Am I living still?'

Hunt at Lake Kariji[18]

Our great Prince who orders
The eight corners of our land,
August Child of the Sun
That shines for us on high,
Lines up his royal horses
And courses this spring day
Over the tender grass
That carpets these high moors.
Even the boar and deer
Bow down their necks in homage.
Even the flying quail
Swoop down and bend to him.
Like boar and stag

We too obey.
Like swooping quail
We too adore.
We serve him and revere.
We lift our eyes up to the brilliant sky,
And there we see
Our mighty Prince,
Young, young as the spring grass
That grows beneath our feet.

Envoy

Our glorious Prince
Has snared the moon
That walks the eternal sky
And makes of it his silken canopy!

On leaving his wife

The thick sea-pine
Grows on the rocks
In the sea of Iwami
Off the Cape of Kara.
The sea-tangle clings
To the rocky beach.
Like the sea-tangle
She bent and clung to me,
My wife, my love; deep
As the deep sea-pine
Was my love for her.
Yet the nights are few
When we have slept together.
The creeping ivy parts,
And we have parted too.
My heart aches when I think
Of her, but when I look
Back, the yellow leaves

Of the mountain flutter and hide
Her distant waving sleeve.
As the moon through a wide rift
Peeps, then hides in the clouds,
My wife is hidden, and I
Grieve. The sun is low.
And I, a strong man —
Or so I thought — make wet
My heavy sleeves with tears.
My glossy steed goes fast,
And far as the clouds I've come
From my wife, from my home.
You yellow leaves that cover
The autumn mountain, cease
Your falling for a while,
For I would see my love.

YOSAMI
wife of Hitomaro

At the death of her husband

Today, today,
I wait for him,
But do not men say
He lies mingled with the shells
Of Stone River?[19]

To meet him face to face —
I may not meet him thus.
Stay, you smoke-clouds[20]
Over Stone River,
That, seeing, I may remember.

HITOMARO KASHŪ
(*Hitomaro Collection*)

Four tanka

1

On the road to the Palace –
Palace basking in the sun –
Men walk in their crowds.
But the man for whom I long
Is one and one alone.

2

'Heaven and earth' –
Only when their names
Become extinct
Would you and I
Meet no more.

3

The silkworms my mother rears –
Mother of the sagging breasts –
Are confined in their cocoons.
My girl, cooped up in her home –
O for a way to meet with her!

4

Clear and loud
As the night call
Of a man of Haya,[21]
I told my name.
Trust me as your wife.[22]

PRINCE HOZUMI

Left at home,
Locked in a chest,
That scoundrel love
Has grasped me again.

TAJIHI

Lamenting his wife's death

In the evening
They bustle by the reeds,
In the morning
They dive offshore:
Even the wild duck
Sleep close by their mates,
Lest on their tails
The hoar-frost fall.
Crossing their wings,
White as the paper-tree,
They sweep it away.
As flowing water
Does not return,
As the wind that blows
Is never seen,
So, without a trace,
Being of this world,
My wife has left in death.
Spreading the lonely sleeves
Of the tattered clothes
She made for me to wear,
I must lie alone.

Envoy

The cranes call
As they cross to the reeds.
Faint and helpless,
Now I lie alone.

ŌTOMO TABITO

In praise of sake

Thirteen tanka

1
Rather than worry
Without result,
One should put down
A cup of rough *sake*.

2
In calling it 'sage',
That splendid sage
Of long ago – how right he was![23]

3
What the Seven Sages, too,[24]
Long ago craved and craved
Was *sake* above all.

4
Rather than be wise
Churning out words,
Better drink your *sake*,
And weep drunken tears.

5
How to speak of it
I know not, yet
The thing I prize
The most is *sake*.

6
Sooner than be a man,
I'd be a *sake* jar,
Soaking in *sake*.[25]

7
O what an ugly sight,
The man who thinks he's wise
And never drinks *sake*!
Give him a good look –
How like an ape he is!

8
Even a priceless jewel –[26]
How can it excel
A cup of rough *sake*?

9
Even jewels that flash
At night – are they like
The draught of *sake*
That frees the mind?

10
Of the ways to play,
In this world of ours,
The one that cheers the heart
Is weeping *sake* tears.

11

If I revel
In this present life,
In the life to come
I may well be a bird,
May well be an insect.[27]

12

'All creatures that live
In the end shall die.'[28]
Well, then, while I live
It's pleasure for me.

13

Calm and knowing ways –
These are not for me.
Instead I'd rather weep
Sake-sodden tears!

Returning to his old home

The empty house
With no one there
Is harder even
Than when I journeyed,
Grass for my pillow.

With my wife,
Together we made it –
Our garden with its streams.
Now the trees we set
Grow too tall and rank.

My wife planted
This plum-tree.
When I look on it
My heart chokes,
And the tears well up.

YAMANOUE OKURA[29]

Poems of the fisherfolk of Shika in Chikuzen

Though not commanded
By our Imperial Lord,
By his own will Arao sailed,
Waving his sleeves as a sign
That the sea was running high.

Soon he must come, we think,
Piling rice high in his bowl.
At the door we stand and wait,
But he does not come.

Spare the trees on Shika Hill –
It was Arao's haunt;
Then, as we look at it,
We may dream of him.

Since the day Arao went
Lonely are the inlets
Fished by the Shika folk.

Heedless of wife and child,
These eight years gone,
We wait for Arao,
But he does not come.

Should the boat
Named *Mallard* pass,
Guard of Yara Cape,
Be swift to tell.

Pining for his son Furuhi

The seven treasures
Prized by man in this world –
What are they to me?

Furuhi, the white pearl
That was born to us,
With dawn's first star
Would not leave our bed,
But, standing or lying,
Played and romped with us.
With dark's evening star,
Linking hand with hand,
'Come to bed,' he would say,
'Father, mother, beside me:
In the middle, I'll sleep,
Like sweet daphne, triple-stalked.'

Such his pretty words.
Soon, for good or ill,
We should see him man –
So we trusted,
As in a great ship.
Then, beyond all thought,
Blowing hard, a sudden crosswind
Overwhelmed him. Lacking skill
And knowing no cure,
With white hemp I tied my sleeves,
Took my mirror in my hand
And, lifting up my eyes,
To the gods in heaven I prayed,
My brow laid on the ground
Doing reverence to the earth spirits.
'Be he ill or be he well,
It is in your power, O gods.'
Thus I clamoured in my prayer.
Yet no good came of it,
For he wasted away,
Each dawn spoke less,
Until his life was ended.
I stood, I jumped, I stamped,
I shrieked, lay on the ground,

I beat my breast and wailed.
Yet the child I held so tight
Has flown beyond my clasp.
Is this our world's way?

Envoys

1

He is too young
To know his way.
Gifts I offer,
Herald of the world below:
O take him on your back.

2

Offerings I make and ask,
Do not deceive him:
Conduct him straight,
Teach the way to heaven.

Dialogue on poverty

On cold nights
When the cold rain beats
And the wind howls,
On cold nights
When the cold snow falls
And the sleet swirls,
My only defence
Against that cold
Is to nibble black salt
And sip *sake* dregs.
But I finger my beard –
Scanty and starved –
Sniffle and cough,
And say to myself
'I'm a good fellow' –

Proud words, and empty:
I freeze all the same,
Swathing myself
In sheets made of sacking,
Piling on the top
My flimsy clothes.
The cold still seeps through.
But there are some
Poorer than I am,
Parents cold and hungry,
Womenfolk and children
Choking on tears.
On cold nights
How do *they* live?

Heaven and earth are broad,
So they say.
For me they are narrow.
Sun and moon are bright,
So they say.
They don't shine for me.
Is it the same for all men,
This sadness?
Or is it for me alone?
Chance made me man
And I, like any other, plough and weed.
But from my clothes –
Thin even when new – tatters hang down
Waving like seaweed.
In my rickety hovel the straw
Lies on bare earth.
By my pillow squat my parents,
At my feet my wife and children:
All huddled in grief.
From the hearth no smoke rises,
In the cauldron
A spider weaves its web.

How do you cook rice
When there is no rice left?
We talk feebly as birds.
And then, to make bad worse,
To snip the ends of a thread
Already frayed and short,
The village headman comes,
Shaking his whip in my face,
Shouting out for his tax,
Right at my pillow.
Is this the way things go?
Must it go on and on?
Yes. We are on earth.

Envoy

Earth is despair and shame.
But I am no bird, and I
Cannot escape from it.

The impermanence of human life

We are helpless in this world.
The years and months slip past
Like a swift stream, which grasps and drags us down.
A hundred pains pursue us, one by one.
Girls, with their wrists clasped round
With Chinese jewels, join hands
And play their youth away.
But time cannot be stopped,
And when their youth is gone
Their jet-black hair, black as a fish's bowels,
Turns white, like a hard frost.
On their sun-browned, glowing faces,
Wrinkles are etched — by whom?

Boys, with their swords at their waists,
Clutching the hunting bow,
Mount their chestnut horses
On saddles linen-spun,
And ride on in their pride.
But is their world eternal?
He pushes back the door
Where a girl sleeps within,
Gropes to her side and lies
Arm on her jewel arm.
But how few are those nights
Before, with stick at waist,
He goes shunned and detested —
The old are always so.
We grudge life moving on
But we have no redress.
I would become as those
Firm rocks that see no change.
But I am a man in time
And time must have no stop.

KASA KANAMURA

On the occasion of the sovereign's visit to Yoshino Palace in summer, fifth month, 725

Like crystal through the mountains —
The broad-shouldered mountains —
Tumbles the Yoshino River.
Pure are its torrents.
In the upper shoals
Plovers cry ceaselessly;
In the lower pools
The frogs call to their mates.
The people of the palace too —

The palace stout-timbered and stoned –
In their throngs walk here and there.
Each time I look at it,
I think how rare the scene is:
Long, long as the jewelled vine,
Never ceasing, for a thousand ages
May it stay so: thus
To the gods of heaven and earth
I pray, in dread of their majesty.

Envoys

1

Though I shall look for a thousand ages
I shall not be wearied:
Our Lord's palace, by the valley
Of the tumbling Yoshino.

2

Will the gods not grant
That man's life, and my own,
Be constant as the rock-bed
Of Yoshino's cascades?

YAMABE AKAHITO

Climbing to Kasuga Moor

High on the peak of Mikasa
Which overtops Kasuga Range,
At every dawn
The clouds billow:
Never stopping
The curlew calls.
Like the clouds
My heart will not settle,

Like the birds
I cry my one-sided love.
All the day and all the night,
Standing, sitting,
I long for her –
The girl I never meet.

Envoy

High on the peak of Mikasa
The birds call.
They cease and they call again:
My love dies, then lives again.

TAKAHASHI MUSHIMARO

For Fujiwara Umakai on his departure in 732 as Inspector of the Western Sea Highway

On Tatsuta Hill
Where white clouds billow
The colours change
With dew and frost.
You cross it on your journey,
Tramping on and on
Over five hundred hills
To reach Tsukushi,
Guarded from raiding foes.
To the limits of the mountains,
To the limits of the plains,
Dividing and dispatching
Your regiments of men:
Even to the ends of the land,
Where the Echo Man responds,
Even to the bounds of water
As far as crawls the toad,

You will go to inspect
The state of your domain.
Then when spring returns
After winter's confining,
Swift as the flying bird
May you come back again.
On Tatsuta Way
As it skirts the hills,
When red azaleas bloom
And cherry blossoms flower,
I shall come forth
To welcome your return.

Though the foe may raise
A thousand, ten thousand men,
To conquer and return
Without a single word –
My lord is such a man.

The maiden of Mama in Katsushika

In the land of Azuma[30]
Where the cocks crow,
Still they tell today
A story of the past:
How the maiden of Mama
In Katsushika
Wove pure hemp
To make herself a skirt
And made a blue collar
For her hempen dress.
Her hair uncombed,
She went unshod, yet
No well guarded damsel,
Cocooned in brocade,
Was ever fair as she.

Her face full as full moon,
Her smile like a flower,
Men sought and crowded round her
As summer moths seek fire,
As boats hurry to port.
Why, when she knew full well
That life is not lived long,
Did her body lie in death
By the sounding estuary
Where sea and river clash?
This happened long ago,
Yet I am made to think
I saw her yesterday.

Envoy

I see the well of Mama[31]
In Katsushika,
And I think of that maid
Who drew water here.

Urashima of Mizunoe

On a misty day in spring,
When I go to Suminoe beach[32]
And see the bobbing fishing smacks,
Things long ago come back to me.

Urashima of Mizunoe,
Elated by his catch
Of bonito and sea bream,
Even after seven days
Did not turn back home,
But rowed beyond the sea's end
And there chanced to meet
The Sea God's daughter.

Entranced by each other,
They spoke, and made their vows,
And, joined as one,
Entered the Eternal Land.

In the palace of the Sea God,
Behind the splendid screens
In his sumptuous halls,
Going hand in hand
They might have dwelt for ever,
Never ageing, never meeting death.
But he, foolish, of our world,
Spoke to his wife and said,
'For a while I shall go home
To speak with my parents, but soon,
Soon as tomorrow, shall return.'

'If you will return
To this Eternal Land,
If we meet as we are now,
Never open this comb casket.'
So she said, and bound him to it.

Coming to Suminoe, he sought
His house and home, but could find none.
Thinking it strange that in the space
Of three years since he left his home
All could be gone, no fence remaining,
'If I open this casket,' he said,
'My old home may be restored.'
So saying, he opened it a little,
When a white cloud swirled from it,
Drifting to the Eternal Land.
He stood, he ran, he shouted, shook his sleeves,
He thrashed and stamped the ground. Then suddenly
His mind went mad. The skin that had been young
Grew furrows, and his black hair turned to white.
Then in time his breath grew faint

And at last his blood ran cold.
Now I look on where it stood,
Urashima of Mizunoe's home.

Envoy

He might have lived
In the Eternal Land.
Yet, of his own doing . . .
O foolish, simple man!

When Lord Ōtomo, the Revenue Officer, climbed Mount Tsukuba

My lord came to survey
The peaks of Tsukuba,
The mountain of black clouds,
In our province of Hitachi.
In the hot summer sun,
The sweat ran down, we panted,
Hauled ourselves up by roots,
Climbed on, our breathing heavy.
Thus we reached the peak
And looked about us, where
The God of the western peak
Revealed his realm below,
The Goddess of the eastern peak
Displayed her magic power.
The crags of Tsukuba's peak,
Shrouded in mist and rain
That always hover there,
Flashed in the brilliant light:
The beauties of our land
That always lay obscured
The gods that moment showed
In shining clarity.

And in our grateful joy
We stripped away our clothes,
Ran and jumped and played
As if we were at home.

Envoys

1

The spring grass bent and swayed.
With summer, it grows rank.
And yet this summer day
Is happier even than spring.

2

What could surpass today?
The day when my father first
Came to Tsukuba's peak?
Even that day grows pale.

KAMO TARUHITO

Mount Kagu

The mists of spring
Hang on Mount Kagu,
The hill that fell from the skies.
Through the pines
The wind rustles
And blows waves across the lake.
Cherry-flowers open,
So thick they shade the tree.
Across the water, the duck
Calls to his mate.
By the shore the teal clamour,
And the boats of the courtiers,
With no oar, no pole,
Lie empty, none to row them.

Envoys

1
Yes, no one to row them.
The duck and teal
There make a home.

2
Unawares, all grew old:
Even the mountain's cypresses, standing like spears,
Grew moss thick at their feet.

THE EMBASSY TO SHIRAGI[33]

Six tanka *exchanged between one who sailed and his wife*

In a creek in Muko Bay
The water-hen folds its wings.
Sundered from you
I shall die for love.
                    [by the wife]

On my lofty ship
Could you, a wife, embark,
Folding my wings over you,
I would sail off.
                    [by the husband]

On the beach where you sleep,
When the sea mist billows
You may know it as like
The breath from my sighing.
                    [by the wife]

When autumn is here
We shall meet again.
Why should you sigh so
Your breath turns to trailing mist?
                    [by the husband]

You who journey to Shiragi,
To see your eyes again,
Today, tomorrow,
I shall wait and fast.
                    [by the wife]

I was not to know
My ship must wait the tide.
O how I regret
Parting from her too soon.
                    [by the husband]

On the journey (*two* tanka)

Looking at the moon on putting out from the shore at Nagato[34]

Behind the mountain ledge
The moon creeps and hides;
The lights of the fishing-boats
Are mirrored over the open sea.

We think our boat is alone
Rowed through the black night:
Then from the open sea
Comes the plash of paddles.

On the journey (chōka)

From Mitsu Beach
Familiar to me as
The morning mirror to my wife,
Fitting many oars
To our great ships,
We set out to cross
To the land of Kara.
We made for Minume
Lying straight ahead,
Piloted through the shallows
As we waited for the tide.
In the open sea
The white-horse waves ran high,
So we rowed along
Hugging the coast,
Past the Isle of Awaji
Wrapped in evening mist.

The night grew dark,
We lost our way
And in Akashi Bay
We stayed our ships,
Our beds tossing
As we slept.
Out at sea we saw
The tiny boats of fishing girls,
Bobbing beacons all in line.

At full tide, with the dawn,
Cranes flew crying to the reeds:
'With the morning calm
We set forth,' called
Helmsman and rower alike.
And like a flock of grebe
We divided the waters

Towards the Home Islands
Dimly lining the horizon.
Thinking to console our hearts,
We rowed our great ships swiftly,
But the billows of the open sea
Stood high in between.

We turned our eyes
And rowed away,
And weighed anchor in Tama Bay.
Looking at the shore,
Like orphans we wailed.
Pearls that deck the Sea God's hand
I gathered for my wife at home;
But with none to bear them back,
To hold them has no point
And I put them down again.

Envoys

1
In Tama Bay
White sea-pearls
I gathered,
Putting them away
With none to see them.

2
When autumn comes
Our ships will return.
Carry grief-forgetting shells
And lodge them here,
White waves of the open sea.

On reaching Buzen (tanka)

The beacons of the fishing-boats
Flashing on the sea-plains;
Make them burn brighter –
I would see the hills of Yamato.

Looking at the moon (tanka)

When evening comes
The autumn wind blows cold.
O that I could go home
And quickly don the clothes
My wife unstitched and washed.

Tanka

I am on a journey
Yet at night I make a fire.
In the dark, my love
Will be pining for me.
   [by Mibu Utamaro, an official of the Embassy]

On the sudden death of Yuki Yakamaro at Iki Island

Our comrade, crossing
To the land of Kara,
To the distant court
Of our Imperial Lord –
Was it that those at home
Waited not in abstinence?
Was it that he himself
Fell into some error?
'When autumn comes
I shall return,'

To his mother he promised —
Mother of the sagging breasts.
That time has passed,
That moon has waned.
Yet, 'Will it be this day,
Will it be tomorrow?'
So saying, those at home
Wait for him and pine.
While he, before he reached
That distant land,
And from Yamato
Sundered far,
Lies on the rock-roots
Of savage island shores.

Envoys

1

You who lie
On Iwata Moor,[35]
Should those at home
Ask where you are,
What words am I to say?

2

The ways of this world
Can never but be so.
Thus are we sundered.
My love for you set at naught,
Must I journey on?

POEMS BY FRONTIER GUARDS AND THEIR FAMILIES

The dreadful order
I have received.
From tomorrow
With the grass I sleep,
No wife being with me.

        [by Mononobe Akimochi]

That wife of mine
Must love me much:
In the water I drink,
Even, her shadow.
I could never forget her.

        [by Wakayama Mimaro]

Behind my parents' house
Grows the centi-grass.
Live a hundred years
Until I shall come back.

        [by Ikutamabe Tarukuni]

O that I'd had
A moment to paint
A picture of my wife.
Looking at it on the journey,
I could have seen and thought.

        [by Mononobe Furumaro]

In the scramble to get away –
Like the waterfowl taking off –
I came not saying a word
To my mother and father,
And now I regret it.

        [by Udobe Ushimaro]

'I shall forget,' I said,
Marching over moor and mountain.
I tell you now, my parents,
I never can forget.

       [by Akinoosa Obitomaro]

You stood at a bend
In that fence of reeds,
Your sleeve sodden with tears.
So I picture you.

       [by Osakabe Ataechikuni]

Staying here at home
Longing for you? No!
Would that I could be
The broad sword you wear
And guard your body.

       [by the father of Kusakabe
           Omininaka, a guard]

The horse is loose
In the mountain pasture.
I couldn't hobble him for life,
So I'll have to send you off
On foot over Tama Brow.

       [by Ojibe Kurome, wife of the
           guard Kurahashibe Aramushi]

'Whose man goes
As frontier guard?'
I hear them ask
With no anxiety –
And how I envy them.

       [by the wife of a guard]

On the road to Yamashiro –
Yamashiro with its rolling hills –
Other wives' men travel on horseback,
While you, my own man, go on foot.
Each time I watch, I can but weep.
I think of it and my heart is pained.
My mother's token that I keep –
Mother of the sagging breasts –
My bright mirror and my shawl,
Thin as the wings of the dragonfly,
Take them, my dear, barter them for a horse.

Envoys

1

The Izumi ford is deep –
Deep enough to drench
My husband's travel clothes.

2

My bright mirror
Means nothing to me
When I see you
On foot, toiling on.

                    [by the wife of a guard]

If I buy a horse,
You must go on foot.
Even should we tramp rough rocks,
I would rather walk with you.

                    [by her husband]

While the leaves of the bamboo rustle
On a cold and frosty night,
The seven layers of clobber I wear
Are not so warm, not so warm
As the body of my wife.

                    [by a guard]

PRINCESS HIROKAWA

The grass of love would load
Seven high harvest carts.
Such grass grows tall, and grows
Heavy on my heart.

LADY HEGURI

A thousand years, you said,
As our hearts melted.
I look at the hand you held,
And the ache is hard to bear.

LADY KASA

Six tanka *written for Yakamochi*

Like the pearl of dew
On the grass in my garden
In the evening shadows,
I shall be no more.

Even the grains of sand
On a beach eight hundred days wide
Would not be more than my love,
Watchman of the island coast.

The breakers of the Ise Sea
Roar like thunder on the shore.
As fierce as they, as proud as they,
Is he who pounds my heart.

I dreamt of a great sword
Girded to my side.
What does it signify?
That I shall meet you?

The bell has rung, the sign
For all to go to sleep.
Yet thinking of my love
How can I ever sleep?

To love a man without return
Is to offer a prayer
To a devil's back
In a huge temple.[36]

LADY KI

For Yakamochi

It was for you, my slave,
That these hands worked so hard.
These reed-ears, plucked
On the spring moors,
Eat them and grow fat.

Flowering when the sun is up,
Sleeping at night as after love,
Should your lady gaze on it alone?
I send this silk tree to him,
That my slave may see it too.

Yakamochi's reply

The slave, it seems,
Loves his lady,
He eats the reed-ears
She deigned to give him,
Yet wastes the more.

The silk tree that
My lady sent
May bear, perhaps,
Flowers alone
And never fruit.

LADY ŌTOMO OF SAKANOUE

Sent from the capital to her elder daughter

More than the gems
Locked away and treasured
In his comb-box
By the God of the Sea,
I prize you, my daughter.
But we are of this world
And such is its way!
Summoned by your man,
Obedient, you journeyed
To the far-off land of Koshi.
Since we parted,
Like a spreading vine,
Your eyebrows, pencil-arched,
Like waves about to break,
Have flitted before my eyes,
Bobbing like tiny boats.
Such is my yearning for you
That this body, time-riddled,
May well not bear the strain.

Envoy

Had I only known
My longing would be so great,
Like a clear mirror
I'd have looked on you —
Not missing a day,
Not even an hour.

Heartburn

Like the sedge of Naniwa,
Naniwa of the glinting waves,
Was his pledge, warm and firm.
'As the years grow thick and fast
So shall I love,' he said.
I granted him my heart,
Clear polished as a mirror;
From that very day
My heart has never wavered,
Swaying like the sea-tangle
That bends back and forth with the waves.
But while I put my trust in him
As in a great ship —
Was it the mighty gods
That sundered us?
Was it man in our world
That came between us?
He that came before
Comes not now to me:
His herald's jewelled bow
Is never to be seen.
But there is no redress.
Through the long night,
Black as leopard-flower,
Until the red sunset
I grieve, with no relief,

I pine, with no device.
'Weak is woman' so men say,
And men are right.
Sobbing, sobbing, like a child,
Pacing always the same path,
I wait for one to bring his news,
And yet none ever comes.

Envoy

From the first
Had he not said, 'For ever',
Causing me to take my faith,
I should not have met
Grief heavy as this.

ŌTOMO YAKAMOCHI

Presented to Lady Ōtomo of Sakanoue's elder daughter

To the pit of my heart I pine,
Not knowing what to say,
Not knowing what to do.

You and I, hands clasped,
That morning stood in the garden:
That night making our bed,
White sleeves intertwined, we slept.
O that it be so always.

The copper pheasant, so men say,
Courts his mate across twin peaks.
I, mere mortal (why must it be so?)
If parted just one day, one night,
Sigh and pine for you.

I think until my breast is bruised,
So (perhaps it will heal my heart)
I ramble Takamado's hills and moors,
But there, seeing only flowers in bloom,
Each time I look I think of you the more.

What should I do
To forget this thing –
This thing with the name 'love'?

In the bindweed flower
On Takamado Moor,
I see my darling's face.
And how could I forget?

Expressing his delight on dreaming of his stray hawk

In the far realm of our Lord,
Named Koshi, where the snow falls,
Distant as are the heavens,
There are tall mountains, grand rivers,
Wide plains, grasses growing lush.
At midsummer, when trout are leaping,
Those who fish with cormorants
By the river's clear shallows,
Lighting torches, make their way upstream.
When autumn came with frost and dew –
As birds began to gather in the fields –
I led forth my comrades with many hawks.
My own Blackie, his tail arrow-pointed,
To which I fastened silver-lacquered bells,
In the dawn hunt set up five hundred,
At the evening beat a thousand birds.
He never lost a chase, and, when let loose,
He swiftly came to wrist again.
If I put him aside, it would be hard
To find another like him. Thus proud at heart

I smiled and spent my days.
Then my crazed old follower, without a word,
Went hawking on a clouded, rain-dark day.
Telling but his name, he said, 'Mishima Moor
At his tail, topping Futagami Peak
He flew till hidden by the clouds.'
Returning, thus he coughed between his words.
I had no means of calling in my hawk,
I found no words that might avail.
Fire even singed my heart, I pined,
I sighed, and then, in hope of finding him,
On the hill slopes I spread catching nets,
I stationed guards. Then to the spirits
I offered a bright mirror and woven cloth.
I prayed and waited; then in a dream
A maiden said to me, 'The fine hawk you pine for
Over Matsudae Beach flew till nightfall,
Crossing Himi Creek where men catch tench,
Then flew over Tako Island. Two days ago, and yesterday,
He was by Furu Creek where reed-duck gather.
He will return before two days have passed
At least, seven days at most. In your heart
Do not languish so.' Thus the maiden spoke.

Envoys

1

The days have grown
And passed to months
Since, hawk on wrist,
I hunted Mishima Moor

2

I spread nets on the slopes
Of Futagami Peak:
The hawk I waited for
Was told me in a dream.

Making fun of a thin man

Iwamaro, look!
Shall I tell you what?
For summer sickness, catch
An eel, and let it cook.
Then – down the hatch!

Ever thinner
Though you be,
Better stay alive.
When you're after eels for dinner,
Watch your step. Don't dive.

Parting sorrows of a frontier guard

In the service of
My mighty Lord,
I set out south
To guard the islands.
My mother, catching up her skirt,
Rubbed it over me as a charm.
My father, with his beard as white
As mulberry-rope, wet it with tears.
He groaned and said,
'My only son,
To leave at dawn!
Long years and months
Must pass before
We meet again.'

My wife spoke too:
'Just for today
Let us talk together.'
So she grieved,
Tender as grass.
My children, too,

Clustered about me,
Wailing and weeping
Like the spring birds.
Sleeves white as mulberry
Sodden with tears,
Tugged at my hands,
Reluctant to part,
Tugged me, and tried
To follow behind.
But my grand Lord's
Command I obeyed,
And followed the road.
At each hill's ridge
I turned to look back
A thousand times.
So I have come
Far from my folk,
And thinking of them
My mind has no ease;
My yearning for them
Burdens my heart.
I am of this world,
Cannot know when I'll die.
'Grant that I may row
The dread sea-way
From island to island,
Go, and return.
And until my return,
May my father and mother
Stay whole and safe;
Free from all ills
May my wife wait.'
To the God of Suminoe,
The seafarer's god,
With sacred wands
I spoke this prayer.

Go. Tell them at home
At Port Naniwa
I equipped my ship,
Fitted many oars,
Made ready my crew
And rowed off at dawn.
The people at home
May well be fasting.
Tell my parents that
My ship is under weigh
And all is calm.

Envoys

1
The cloud that sails
The distant sky
Men call a messenger.
Yet no messenger can
Bear gifts to my home.

2
As gifts for my home
I gathered sea-shells.
But the waves reach up
And beat on the shore.

3
In the lee of an island
Our ship is anchored.
But to carry this news
I can find no herald.
Longing in vain,
I must sail on.

Heian Period
(794–1185)

ONO TAKAMURA

Masked by the snowflakes,
The colour of your petals
May well be hidden:
Yet still put forth your scent
That men may know you flower.

ARIWARA NARIHIRA

Eight extracts from Ise Monogatari

I

A lady lived in the western apartments of the palace of the Empress Dowager when it was in Gojō[37] in the eastern part of the capital. Narihira visited her there, at first thinking little of it, but then, on some account, became more intimate with her. However, on about the tenth day of the first month, the lady moved elsewhere; he heard where she was, but as the place was not one he might frequent himself, he passed his days in dark gloom. In the first month of the following year, with the plum-flowers at their full, recalling fondly the happiness of the previous year, he went again to the western apartments. But though he stood and gazed, sat and gazed and looked all about him, the place had an entirely different feeling. Saddened and hurt at heart, with no door, no screen to protect him, he lay prostrate on the bare boards until the moon sank in the west.

Remembering the events of the previous year, he wrote:

Can it be that the moon has changed?
Can it be that the spring
Is not the spring of old times?
Is it my body alone
That is just the same?

2

After the rite of his initiation into manhood, Narihira went down on a ceremonial hawking hunt to the village of Kasuga, near the old capital of Nara, where his estates lay. In the village lived two sisters of striking beauty. Peeping through a hole in their fence, his heart was disturbed and arrested when he reflected on such unlooked-for loveliness in such ill-fitting and rustic surroundings. Cutting the skirt of his hunting-cloak, which was in a pattern of passion plant, he wrote a poem on it and sent it to them.

> Seeing such blooming beauty,
> Fresh as the *murasaki* of Kasuga Moor,
> Like this passion-plant pattern,
> The passion in my heart
> Knows not any limit.

This poem must have been found appropriate and fascinating, for its spirit is the same as that of the poem

> Like a passion-plant pattern
> Is my heart tangled.
> Who was it brought this tangle?
> For it was not my doing.

So nimble and responsive to the occasion was the taste of the ancients.

3

In former times Narihira travelled to Ise as the Imperial Envoy at the Ceremonial Falconry. The Princess who was acting then as vestal at the Grand Shrine was told by her mother that she must receive him with greater solicitude and kindness than was accorded to the ordinary envoy. As this was her mother's word, she entertained her guest with the utmost concern for his well-being. In the morning she supervised the arrangements for the falcon hunt and at his return in the evening she had him come to her own apartment. On the night of the second day, the envoy said that he wished very much to meet her – a meeting which she found by no means repugnant, yet which, because of the number of prying eyes, she feared it would be difficult to arrange. However, in that he was leading the delegation, Narihira had been lodged in the innermost part of the apartments, near to the quarters of the Princess herself. At midnight that night, when all were sound asleep, the Princess went to him. Narihira, too, lay sleepless, looking out beyond his room; through the misty moonlight he saw her standing there, a small girl in front of her. Overjoyed he led her to his bed, where she stayed for some hours, but was obliged to return before they had been able to talk to the full.

Sorrowful, he stayed sleepless for the rest of the night. In the morning, his heart filled with yearning, he could find no cheer, and, as he might not himself send anyone to communicate with her, he could only wait anxious and impatient. At last, soon after dawn, there came from her a simple poem with no message attached:

Was it you who came to me
Or I who went to you —
I know not.
Was it dream or reality,
Sleeping or awake?

Weeping, Narihira made his verse:

In the blackness
Of a numbed heart,
I lost my way.
Dream or reality —
Let other men decide.

Narihira then set out for the hunt. Yet as he walked over the moors his thoughts were inattentive and all he could think of was his longing to be with her again that night when all were asleep. However, the Provincial Governor of Ise, who, in addition, had supervision of the vestals, hearing that the Envoy to the Hunt had arrived, invited him to a banquet which lasted through the night. Narihira was thus quite unable to meet her and since he must needs depart with the daylight for the province of Owari, he shed secret, sorrowing tears. But they were of no avail.

Just as it began to grow light, there came from her the cup of leave-taking in which was written a poem:

Shallow our union,
Shallow as the inlet
One walks unwetted.

The final couplet was missing. Narihira wrote it in on the wine-cup, using the tip of a charred pine-torch,

Over the Barrier of Meeting Hill
Again I shall climb to you.[38]

4

Once a man, tired of living in the capital, went to the Eastland. As he travelled along the coast between Ise and Owari, he noticed the white of the breakers and recited this poem:

More and more
Do I yearn for
The capital I have left.
O how I envy
Waves that can return.

5

On the occasion of the archery contest of the Right Troop of the Inner Palace Guard on the sixth day of the fifth month, a maiden's face could be dimly discerned through the curtains of a carriage that stood at the opposite side of the arena. Captain Narihira composed this poem and sent it to her:

It was not that I could not see her,
Yet I did not see her clearly.
Longing for her,
Fruitlessly I shall spend
This long day lost in thought.

The woman replied to this with:

To know or not to know –
Why should we make
This vain distinction?
This deep longing
Alone is love's beacon.

Later he came to know who she was.

6

Once there was an extremely honest and upright man with never a fickle thought for anyone. He was in service to Emperor Fukakusa and must indeed have been under a delusion when he allowed himself to exchange pledges with a maiden who served the Imperial Princess.

So he sent her this poem:

> The dream of the night
> We slept together
> Is fleeting.
> Now that I drowse
> It is even more fleeting.

What a shabby and ignoble poem!

7

Once there lived a woman in the western part of the capital. She was more beautiful than any in the world but even so the grace of her heart outshone that of her appearance. But it seemed that she was not without a lover. Having spoken tender words of love to her, and back in his home, what might have been the thoughts of our upright and honest man? In early March, the spring drizzle falling softly, he sent her this poem:

> Tossing in my bed
> The whole night through,
> Neither waking nor sleeping,
> It is a thing of spring,
> This long rain haze
> At which I gaze so long.[39]

8

Once a man who had decided that he was of service to no one resolved not to stay on in the capital and to seek somewhere to live in the Eastland. He set out with one or two old friends as companions. None of the company knew the route and they wandered lost as far as a place called Yatsuhashi – Eight Bridges – in Mikawa province. The name derives from the eight bridges built to span the rivers that fork like spiders' legs and drain the water from a large marsh in that

area. They dismounted by the edge of the marsh and ate a meal of
dried rice in the shade of a tree. In the marsh, iris flowers were
blooming prettily. One of the group, on seeing the flowers, said,
'Would you make a travel poem, each line beginning with the syllables
of the name of this flower?' So he recited:

I   In the capital is the one I love, like
R   Robes of stuff so precious, yet now threadbare.
I   I have come far on this journey,
S   Sad and tearful are my thoughts.

All were moved by this same sadness and wept, their tears falling on
the dried rice and making it sodden . . .

They continued on their journey and came to a wide river, called
the Sumida, which divides the provinces of Musashi and Shimōsa.
As they stood in a listless huddle on the bank, thinking sadly about
the great distance they had come, the ferryman shouted at them,
'Come aboard quickly, for the sun is setting.' They went on board
and were about to cross, each of them thinking forlornly about his
friends and dear ones in the capital. It chanced that just at the time
a bird was sporting on the water and eating fish. The size of a snipe,
it had white feathers and a red beak and legs. It was not a bird known
in the capital so that, as they were none of them familiar with it, they
asked the ferryman, who replied, 'This is the Capital Bird.' Hearing
this, one of them recited:

If you are true to your name,
Then let me question you,
Bird of the Capital,
Of the one I love –
Is she alive or gone?

This affected all who were in the boat so deeply that they wept.

BISHOP HENJŌ

Blow wind of heaven,
Blow and block
The paths of the clouds,
That the sight of these girls
May stay a little.[40]

The lotus, its flowers
Unstained by mud –
So pure in heart.
Why should it pass off
Its dewdrops as jewels?

In fondness for your name alone
I plucked at your stem,
O maiden flower.
Do not tell men
That this was my fall.

When flowers fall,
They turn to dust:
Heedless, the butterfly
Flutters among them.

ARIWARA YUKIHIRA

I must depart now.
But, like the pine
At the peak of Inaba,
Should I hear you pine for me
I shall return to you.

The robe of mist
Worn by the spring –
How thin the weft:
By the mountain wind
So soon disordered!

ŌSHIKŌCHI MITSUNE

I must seek as I pick,
For the first frost lies
Too deep to pick out
White chrysanthemum flowers.

The end of my journey
Was still far off,
But in the tree-shade
Of the summer mountain
I stood, my mind floating.

The blowing wind –
Why should they hate it?
Plum-flowers, when they fall,
Smell their sweetest.

At the great sky
I gaze all my life:
For the rushing wind,
Though it howls as it goes,
Can never be seen.

SUGAWARA MICHIZANE

When the east wind blows,
Send me your perfume,
Blossoms of the plum:
Though your lord be absent,
Forget not the spring.[41]

ANONYMOUS POEMS
from *Kokinshū*

Grass of Kasuga Moor –
Do not burn it, this one day:
My wife, tender as young leaves,
And I lie there together.

I smell the smell
Of the orange-flowers
That wait till May to bloom.
And I picture a friend's sleeve,
A friend I knew so well.

When the moonlight
Starts to seep
Through the trees,
Autumn has come
With trouble, with care.

It grows dark, it seems,
With the cicada shriek.
But it is the walls
Of the mountain cleft
That make the gloom.

May our friend endure
A thousand, eight thousand ages:
Till the smallest pebble grows
To a boulder etched with moss.

If I had known
That old age would call,
I'd have shut my gate,
Replied 'Not at home!'
And refused to meet him.

In this world is there
One thing constant?
Yesterday's depths
In Asuka River
Today are but shallows.

To plant plum-flowers
So near to my home
Showed no taste in me –
Taken for the scent
Of the one I wait for.

Whether you might come
Or I go to you –
As I wavered,
My door unlocked,
I fell asleep.

Beating their wings
Against the white clouds,
You can count each one
Of the wild geese flying:
Moon, an autumn night.

When a thousand birds
Twitter in spring
All things are renewed:
I alone grow old.

In the spring haze
Dim, disappearing,
The wild geese are calling
Above autumn's mist.

Dimly in the dawn mist
Of the Bay of Akashi,
Hidden by islands
I dream of a boat.

MIBU TADAMINE

Since that parting
When she seemed as unfeeling
As the moon at morning,
Nothing so cruel
As the light of dawn.

When the wind blows,
The white clouds are cleft
By the peak. Is your heart,
Like them, so cold?

MINAMOTO MUNEYUKI

In my mountain hamlet
Winter is even more lonely
And forlorn, for man
And grass both wither.

KI TSURAYUKI

Now, I cannot tell
What my old friend is thinking:
But the petals of the plum
In this place I used to know
Keep their old fragrance.

When I went to visit
The girl I love so much,
That winter night
The river blew so cold
That the plovers were crying.

We drink with palms cupped
At the mountain spring
And cloud the still pool.
I drink but, still thirsty,
I must travel on.[42]

Summer night –
I close my eyes
And the cuckoo
With its one cry
Marks the dawn.

I crossed the spring mountains –
Spring of the catalpa bow –
And the track could not be cleared
So many flowers had fallen.

As if it were a relic
Of the cherry-flowers
Scattered by the storm,
In a waterless sky
A wave billowed.

LADY ISE

Forsaking the mists
That rise in the spring,
Wild geese fly off.
They have learned to live
In a land without flowers.[43]

TAIRA KANEMORI

I would conceal it, yet
In my looks it is shown –
My love, so plain
That men ask of me
'Do you not brood on things?'

ONO KOMACHI

The lustre of the flowers
Has faded and passed,
While on idle things
I have spent my body
In the world's long rains.

Was it that I went to sleep
Thinking of him,
That he came in my dreams?
Had I known it a dream
I should not have wakened.

How helpless my heart!
Were the stream to tempt,
My body, like a reed
Severed at the roots,
Would drift along, I think.

When my love becomes
All-powerful,
I turn inside out
My garments of the night,[44]
Night dark as leopard-flower.

BUNYA YASUHIDE

The grasses and trees
Change their colours;
But to the wave-blooms
On the broad sea-plain
There comes no autumn.

ŌNAKATOMI YOSHINOBU

The fires lit by the guards
At the Imperial Palace gates,
Blazing bright by night,
Are damped down at daybreak:
So smoulder my heart's thoughts.

On Evergreen Hill
Where no tree turns crimson,
The deer that haunt there
By their own belling
May know autumn has come.

MINAMOTO SHIGEYUKI

Making no sound
Yet smouldering with passion
The firefly is still sadder
Than the moaning insect.

SONE YOSHITADA

Like a boatman
Crossing Yura Strait,
His rudder gone,
I know not the goal
Of this path of love.

PRIEST NŌIN

I left the capital
Wrapped in spring mist.
But the autumn wind blows
At the White River Barrier.[45]

MINAMOTO TOSHIYORI

The wind howling through the pines –
The forlorn feeling of autumn;
Women fulling cloth
In a hamlet by the Tama River.[46]

FUJIWARA MOTOTOSHI

At the end of autumn,
When the insect voices cease
Over the withering heath,
I would have him ask,
'Is he alive or dead?'

EMPEROR SUTOKU

The swift rapids
Are blocked by a rock,
Yet, though the stream
Is sundered, in the end
It unites again.

The blossom to the roots,
The birds to their old nests,
All have returned.
Yet no man knows
Where spring has gone.

KAGURA
(*'God-music'*)

On the leaves of the bamboo-grass
Snow falls, piles up.
On a winter night,
To make fine music
To the gods is pleasing.

From the first age
Of the timeless gods
We have held
The leaf of the bamboo-grass.

Silver clasp
On his sword
Slung proudly at his thigh,
As he swaggers down
The broad walks of Nara:
Who might he be?

O for a mighty sword,
Mighty as Furu's
Shrine above the Stone![47]
I'd plait thread to thong
And so I would lord it
Down the Royal Palace Way.

AZUMA ASOBI UTA
('*Play-songs of the Eastland*')

Suruga Dance

Ah! On Udo beach,
On Udo beach in Suruga,
The waves fall and plash.
My girl, pretty as
The seven precious stones,
Beautiful from head to toe
Beautiful from head to toe . . .
My girl, pretty as
The seven precious stones,

When we come together
Let us lie as one.
Ah! My girl, pretty as
The seven precious stones,
Beautiful from head to toe.

RYŌJIN HISHŌ

May the man who gained my trust yet did not come
Turn to a devil, sprouting triple horns.
Then he would find himself shunned by mankind.

May he become a bird of the water-paddy
With frost and snow and hailstones raining down.
Then he would find his feet were frozen fast.

May he become the duckweed on the pond.
Then he would sway and shiver as he walked.

Even the moon
Each time it rises
Is young.
What will become
Of my body so full
Of years?

Dance, dance, little snail!
If you do not dance,
I shall have you kicked and crushed
By a pony, by a calf.
If you dance your dance
Well and prettily,
I shall let you go and play
In a garden full of flowers.

A hundred days, a hundred nights,
Though I sleep alone,
What need have I
Of another's wife?
I would not wish it.
From dusk till midnight
Is all very well,
But cock-crow at dawn
Makes the bed feel bare.

The brocade sedge-hat you loved –
O dear, it fell, it fell
Midstream in Kamo River.[48]
I searched for it, I sought so hard,
That day dawned, that day dawned
On that silky autumn night.

The young man come to manhood
Came to claim his bride.
The first night and the second
They slept a deep sound sleep.
Then, the third midnight,
And long before the dawn,
He grabbed his trousers in his hand
And fled far out of sight.

Oh, my man is so unfeeling!
Had he said he hated me,
Or could not bear to live with me,
I might detest and loathe him.
Oh! this bond and tie with parents –
A bond he cannot cut or slip.

[by the bride]

My child is still not twenty,
Yet he travels the land, a gambler.
He gambles in every province,

Yet – my child as he still is –
I cannot come to scold him.
Spirit of Sumiyoshi Shrine, I pray,[49]
Never let him lose his game!

HEIKE MONOGATARI
(*Tale of the Heike*)

Moon-viewing

In this palace there lived also a lady-in-waiting who went by the name of 'Night-awaiting Maid'.

This nickname arose from an incident when the Emperor asked, 'Which is the more saddening – the evening as you wait for him, or the morning when he has gone home?' To this she replied:

'As I wait for him to come,
Now the night grows deep,
The toll of the bell is sadder
Than the crow of the cock
As he leaves at dawn.'

Once the Chamberlain called this maiden, and after they had talked over many things from the past and the present, when the night was growing late, he made a song in the 'present mode' on the topic of the old capital gone to ruin:

We come and we see
The capital of old,
Desolate as a swamp
Unkempt with wild reeds.
The light of the moon
Streams in unshaded:
The wind of autumn
Pierces my bones.

Three times he sang this song with such intensity and feeling that the Empress and all her ladies-in-waiting wet their sleeves through with their tears.

Presently, with the dawn, the Chamberlain made his farewells and set out to return to Fukuhara.[50] He summoned an archivist and said to him: 'I wonder what that lady-in-waiting had on her mind? For she seemed much distressed at our parting. Return and speak a few words to her.'

The archivist hurried back and said, 'These are the words of the Chamberlain:

'"What is it to me?"
You said of the cock-crow
At the dawn parting.
Yet this morning
Seemed to sadden you.'

Straight away she replied:

'When you wait for one to come,
The bell as the night deepens
Is cheerless; yet the dawn cock
That sunders our oneness
Brings greater sorrow.'

The archivist hurried back to report what had taken place. 'You did well; for it was in hopes of such a turn of events that I sent you,' praised the Chamberlain. From that day, the archivist came to be known as the 'What-is-it-to-me?' archivist.

Presently they heard the toll of the bell of the Jakkōin[51] announcing the end of this day too. As the evening sun tilted in the west, although aware that his farewells were not fully said, the Former Emperor, biting back his tears, set out on his return. His Empress found herself recalling former times and was unable to stem the flood of tears with her dabbing sleeve. She watched as his retinue receded farther and farther into the distance, then, going back into her hermitage, she turned to face the Buddha and prayed: 'Grant that the Spirit of the Former Emperor attain perfect enlightenment; that the lost spirits of the entire Taira clan swiftly attain the Way.'

Dwelling with longing on her former life, she wrote verses on the paper of the partition doors of her hermitage:

Oh! these days,
How my sad heart
Slips back to the past,
Yearning for those I knew
In the palace of old.

My life in former days
Has become misted,
As of a dream.
So may this home of woven reeds
Grow old into my past.

Then Sanesada, who had come as one of the Former Emperor's retinue, wrote on the pillar of the hermitage:

In former times
Her beautiful features
Shone like the moon:
Now, murky solitude
Deep in a mountain cleft.

The Empress continued to meditate, now choking on her tears as she thought of the past, now joyful as she contemplated what was to be. Then a cuckoo called twice, three times, as it flew by, and she made this verse:

Come, then, cuckoo,
Let us join our tears
To make a single sob.
I, too, in this world of woes,
Live on, only to weep.

IMAYŌ

The Buddha himself
Was once man like us:
We too at the end
Shall become Buddha.
All creatures may share
The nature of Buddha.
How grievous indeed
That this is not known!

Rather than the vows
Of the myriad Buddhas,
The testament of
The thousand-handed *Kannon*[52]
Has the greater faith,
Powerful in making
The flowers to blossom,
The fruits to ripen,
In a twinkling on limbs
Of trees that are rotten.

Kamakura and Muromachi Periods

(1185–1603)

TAIRA TADANORI

The capital at Shiga,
Shiga of the rippling waves,
Lies now in ruins:
The mountain cherries
Stay as before.

Overtaken by the dark,
The shade beneath a tree
I make my inn;
And tonight my host
Shall be a flower.

PRIEST SHUNE

With the spring, now
They huddle in the mist,
The hills of Awaji,
Seen over the waves
Till yesterday.

PRIEST SAIGYŌ

Trailing on the wind,
The smoke from Mount Fuji
Melts into the sky.
So too my thoughts –
Unknown their resting-place.

At the roadside
Where a clear stream bubbles
In the shade of the willows,
'Just for a while,' I said,
And still have not gone.

A man who has grown distant –
Why should I detest him?
There was a time when,
Unknown, I did not know him.

A man without feelings,
Even, would know sadness
When snipe start from the marshes
On an autumn evening.

Is it a shower of rain?
I thought as I listened
From my bed, just awake.
But it was falling leaves
Which could not stand the wind.

I cannot accept
The real as real:
Then how do I accept
A dream as a dream?

On Mount Yoshino
I shall change my route
From last year's broken-branch trail,
And in parts yet unseen
Seek the cherry-flowers.

The winds of spring
Scattered the flowers
As I dreamt my dream.
Now I awaken,
My heart is disturbed.

The cry of the crickets,
As the nights grow chill
And autumn advances,
Grows weak and more distant.

Every single thing
Changes and is changing
Always in this world.
Yet with the same light
The moon goes on shining.

FUJIWARA SANESADA

The cuckoo called:
I looked towards the sound,
But only the moon
Of the dawn was there.

PRINCESS SHIKISHI

O my soul, my string of gems,
If the string must snap, let it be now:
For, if it endures longer,
My hiding of my love
Must surely grow weaker.

PRIEST JAKUREN

The drops of pattering rain
Are not dry on the cypress leaves
Before trailing mists swirl
On an autumn evening.

Now spring's over, I know not
Where its harbour will be.
Out of sight in the haze
Go the river's firewood barges.

One cannot ask loneliness
How or where it starts.
On the cypress-mountain,
Autumn evening.

FUJIWARA SHUNZEI (TOSHINARI)

Has it flown away,
The cuckoo that called
Waking me at midnight?
Yet its song seems
Still by my pillow.

In autumn, lodging at a temple near his wife's grave

Even at midnight,
When I come so rarely,
The sad wind through the pines:
Must she hear it always
Beneath the moss?

Oh, this world of ours —
There is no way out!
With my heart in torment
I sought the mountain depths,
But even there the stag cries.

MINAMOTO KANEMASA

How many nights have you wakened,
Watchman of the Suma Barrier,
At the screams of the plover
Making back to Awaji Island?

FUJIWARA YOSHITSUNE

No man lives now
In the warden's house
By the Fuwa Barrier,
Its timbers rotten:
Only autumn's winds.

The cicada shrieks
This frosty night:
Spreading my sleeve
On the chilly mat,
I must sleep alone.

KUNAIKYŌ

By the light or dark
Of the green in the fields
Where young shoots sprout,
It can clearly be seen
Where the snow thawed first.

Bringing flowers with it,
Hira's mountain squall
Swept over the lake.
A boat, rowed through,
Left flowers in its wake.

LADY SANUKI

The sleeve of my dress,
Like a rock in the open sea,
Unseen, unknown to man,
Even when the tide ebbs,
Is never for a moment dry.

MINAMOTO SANETOMO

When mountains are split
And the seas run dry –
Should such a world be born,
I would not show a double heart
In the service of my Lord.

The breakers of the ocean
Pound and thunder on the rocks,
Smashing, breaking, cleaving,
They crash upon the shore.

That it might be so always,
This world of ours —
These tiny fisherboats
Rowed close to the beach
With their nets dragging —
Splendid to see!

EMPEROR GOTOBA

Faintly the spring, it seems,
Has come to the sky.
Over Mount Kagu, dropped from heaven,
The mist trails.

Though the nightingale sings,
The leaves of the cedars
Are white with snow still
Here at the mountain meeting-barrier.[53]

FUJIWARA TEIKA (SADAIE)

Pining for one who does not come,
Like the seaweed burnt for salt
In the evening calm of Pine Sail Creek,
My whole body smoulders.

This spring night
The floating bridge of my dream
Fell apart:
Swirling away from the peak,
Dawn clouds in the eastern sky.

As far as the eye can see,
No cherry-blossom,
No crimson leaf:
A thatched hut by a lagoon,
This autumn evening.

He for whom I wait
Comes by a path that skirts the hills,
Which must by now be blocked;
For on the cedar by the eaves
The snow lies heavy.

MUROMACHI BALLADS

On the under-leaves
Of the arrowroot
Shrivelled by frost,
The grasshopper screeches,
Screeches, sorrowing.

The nightingale,
From singing
Grown thin:
I, from awaiting
Him I love,
Grown thin.

Rain beating down
On top of snow.
Add any more and my heart
Melts, melts, melts.

Dropped the door-bolt thong
And rammed it home,
Rammed it home:
Jealous as ever,
She rammed it home.

Men's hearts, like the nets
Of Katada's fishermen,[54]
Are best drawn in the night,
Best drawn in the night.
In the light of day, men's eyes
Are everywhere watching.

The moon shines over the hill field:
His boat puts out to sea off Akashi.
Shine clear, moon; in the mist
The night-boat flounders.
Night, night, black midnight:
And the call of the deer.

The slave-boat rides the open sea:
Here, one who yearns to sell –
But ride me gently, captain!

ARAKIDA MORITAKE

Fallen flower I see
Returning to its branch –
Ah! a butterfly.

Summer night –
Sun wide awake:
My eyelids closed.

As the morning glory
Today appears
My span of life.

YAMAZAKI SŌKAN

Folding its hands
And offering its song,
The bullfrog.

If it rains,
Come with your umbrella,[55]
Midnight moon.

Edo Period

(1603–1868)

MATSUNAGA TEITOKU

Dumplings before cherries[56]
He says, and back he goes,
The wild goose.

YASUHARA TEISHITSU

Oh! oh! is all I can say
For the cherries that grow
On Mount Yoshino.

MATSUO BASHŌ

The sea dark,
The call of the teal
Dimly white.

The cuckoo —
Its call stretching
Over the water.

On a bare branch
A rook roosts:
Autumn dusk,

Seven sights were veiled
In mist — then I heard
Mii Temple's bell.[57]

The beginning of art —
The depths of the country
And a rice-planting song.

Summer grasses —
All that remains
Of soldiers' visions.[58]

Ailing on my travels,
Yet my dream wandering
Over withered moors.

Spring:
A hill without a name
Veiled in morning mist.

Clouds now and then
Giving men relief
From moon-viewing.

The beginning of autumn:
Sea and emerald paddy
Both the same green.

Silent and still: then
Even sinking into the rocks,
The cicada's screech.

To the sun's path
The hollyhocks lean
In the May rains.

Soon it will die,
Yet no trace of this
In the cicada's screech.

The winds of autumn
Blow: yet still green
The chestnut husks.

You say one word
And lips are chilled
By autumn's wind.

A flash of lightning:
Into the gloom
Goes the heron's cry.

Still baking down –
The sun, not regarding
The wind of autumn.

MUKAI KYORAI

Winter blast –
Rain-storm even
Not reaching the ground.

Which is tail? Which head?
Unsafe to guess
Given a sea-slug.

My native town
And in a borrowed bed:
Migrating birds.

NAITŌ JŌSŌ

'I've seen it all,
Down the pond's bottom' –
The look on the duckling's face.

Its sloughed-off shell
At its side in death –
Autumn cicada.

HATTORI RANSETSU

Painting pines
On the blue sky,
The moon tonight.

New Year's Day
Dawns clear, and sparrows
Tell their tales.

Harvest moon,
And mist creeping
Over the water.

ENOMOTO KIKAKU

Harvest moon:
On the bamboo mat
Pine-tree shadows.

Baby sparrows:
On the paper window,
Shadows of dwarf bamboo.

On New Year's dawn,
Sedately, the cranes
Pace up and down.

Wooden gate,
Lock firmly bolted:
Winter moon.

NOZAWA BONCHŌ

Overnight
My razor rusted –
The May rains.

Cool and fresh;
Dawn-cut grass carried
Through the gate.

Brushwood bones
Pruned and lopped,
Yet budding branches.

Winter rain:
A farmhouse piled with firewood,
A light in the window.

MORIKAWA KYOROKU

'Long, long ago now' –
Telling of that earthquake
Round a brazier.

Autumn so soon:
Drizzling on the crags,
First tinted maples.

KONISHI RAIZAN

Girls planting paddy:
Only their song
Free of the mud.

Spring breeze –
How white the heron
Among the pines!

SUGIYAMA SAMPŪ

Glint of hoe
Lifted high up:
Fields in summer.

Cherries, cuckoo,
Moon, snow – soon
The year's vanished.

UEJIMA ONITSURA

Daybreak –
On the corn shoots
White frost of spring.

It's summer; then
'Oh, let's have winter,'
Some men say.

Will there be any
Not wielding his brush?
The moon tonight.

To know the plums,
Own your heart
And own your nose.

Come, come, I say;
But the firefly
Goes on his way.

They bloom and then
We look and then they
Fall and then . . .

Trout leaping:
On the river-bed
Clouds floating.

Green cornfield:
A skylark soaring,
There – swooping.

KUROYANAGI SHŌHA

A heavy cart rumbles,
And from the grass
Flutters a butterfly.

Deep in the temple
The sounds of bamboo-cutting:
Cold evening shower.

TAN TAIGI

'It's the east wind blowing,'
They say as they walk,
Master and servant.

The bridge broken
And men on the bank:
Summer moon.

On the dust-heap
Morning glory flowering:
Late autumn.

A chilling moon
As I walk alone:
Clatter of the bridge.

Winter withering:
Sparrows strut
In the guttering.

MIURA CHORA

You watch – it's clouded;
You don't watch, and it's clear –
When you view the moon.

Peering at the stars
Through its gaps between branches,
The lonely willow.

YOSA BUSON

Scampering over saucers –
The sound of a rat.
Cold, cold.

Spring rain:
Telling a tale as they go,
Straw cape, umbrella.

Spring rain:
In our sedan
Your soft whispers.

Sudden shower:
Grasping the grass-blades
A shoal of sparrows.

Spring rain:
A man lives here –
Smoke through the wall.

Mosquito-buzz
Whenever honeysuckle
Petals fall.

Fuji alone
Left unburied
By young green leaves.[59]

Spring rain:
Soaking on the roof
A child's rag ball.

ŌSHIMA RYŌTA

Night growing late:
Sound of charcoal
Broken on charcoal.

Oh, this hectic world —
Three whole days unseen,
The cherry blossom!

Bad-tempered, I got back:
Then, in the garden,
The willow-tree.

I look at the light:
Yes, there is a wind,
This night of snow.

TAKAI KITŌ

Winter copse:
The moon piercing
To the very marrow.

KATŌ GYŌDAI

Snow melting!
Deep in the hill-mist
A crow cawing.

I light the lamp
And even the back
Of the plum-flowers is seen.

Autumn hills:
Here and there
Smoke is rising.

Mournful wind:
Night after night
The moon wanes.

TAKAKUWA RANKŌ

Rain of a winter storm:
Horns locked as they jostle,
Oxen in the meadow.

ŌTOMO ŌEMARU

Fall on, frost!
After the chrysanthemum
No more flowers.

KOBAYASHI ISSA

The world of dew is
A world of dew . . . and yet,
And yet . . .

My home, where all I touch,
Or try, bears as bloom
A briar.

Thin little frog,
Don't give in:
Issa is here, you know.[60]

Stop! don't swat the fly
Who wrings his hands,
Who wrings his feet.

Melting snow:
And on the village
Fall the children.

The garden: a butterfly.
The baby creeps, it flies.
She creeps, it flies.

Beautiful, seen through holes
Made in a paper screen:
The Milky Way.

With bland serenity
Gazing at the far hills:
A tiny frog.

Emerging from the nose
Of Great Buddha's statue:[61]
A swallow comes.

Slowly, slowly, climb
Up and up Mount Fuji,
O snail.

Far-off mountain peaks
Reflected in its eyes:
The dragonfly.

For fleas, also, the night
Must be so very long,
So very lonely.

Red sky in the morning:
Does it gladden you,
O snail?

Someone, somewhere – there's
Something about that face . . .[62]
That's it – the viper!

The radish-picker
With his radish
Points the way.

Three ha'pence worth
Of fog I saw
Through the telescope.

A world of dew:
Yet within the dewdrops –
Quarrels.

Viewing the cherry-blossom:
Even as they walk,
Grumbling.

Spring rain:
The uneaten ducks[63]
Quack.

BASHŌ, KYORAI, BONCHŌ, FUMIKUNI

The Kite's Feathers [64]

1. (Kyorai) The kite's feathers
Unruffled – first rain
Of early winter.

2. (Bashō) One blast of wind,
Then the leaves are lulled.

3. (Bonchō) His working-breeches
Drenched at dawn,
Fording the stream.

4. (Fumikuni) To scare off badgers,
Bamboo branches bent into bows.

5. (Bashō) Over the door-frame
Creeps the ivy;
Evening moon.

6. (Kyorai) Won't give them to a soul –
His famous pears.

7. (Fumikuni) Revelling in the ink
Drawings he dashes off –
End of autumn.

8. (Bonchō) Comfortable to wear,
His knitted socks.

9. (Kyorai) All things
Silent:
Peace and quiet.

10. (Bashō) They see their first village
And blow the noon conch.

11. (Bonchō) All in tatters,
              Last year's sleeping mats
              Dirty and frayed.

12. (Fumikuni) The lotus petals
               Flutter and fall.

13. (Bashō)   For soup
              To start with, tasty
              Suizenji laver.

14. (Kyorai) It's seven miles and more
              The road I must travel.

15. (Fumikuni) This spring, too,
               Rodō's man
               Stays on.

16. (Bonchō) The cutting takes root:
              Misted moon night.

17. (Bashō)   Moss-grown,
              By the cherry-flowers
              A stone water-stand.

18. (Kyorai) Vanished of itself,
              Morning's flare of passion.

19. (Bonchō) At one sitting
              Two days' food
              He puts away.

20. (Fumikuni) Cold enough for snow
               Island in the north wind.

21. (Kyorai) To light the lamp
              At dusk, climbing
              To the peak temple.

22. (Bashō)   The cuckoos
              All silent now.

23. (Fumikuni)   Skin and bones –
                 For standing up
                 Still no strength.

24. (Bonchō)   Borrowing the neighbour's yard,
                 The carriage is taken in.

25. (Bashō)   Let my man
                 Make his escape
                 By the quince hedge.

26. (Kyorai)   On the point of parting,
                 She gives him the forgotten sword.

27. (Bonchō)   Impatiently
                 She combs
                 Her tangled hair.

28. (Fumikuni)   Look at her, scheming,
                 Shameless in her lust.

29. (Kyorai)   The blue sky:
                 Pale moon in
                 A wan dawn.

30. (Bashō)   Mirrored in the autumn lake,
                 Hira's first frost.

31. (Fumikuni)   By the brushwood gate
                 Writing his verse on
                 The buckwheat thief.

32. (Bonchō)   Getting used to his wadded clothes
                 Now that the evening wind blows cold.

33. (Bashō)   Crowding together
                 As they sleep, then setting out
                 From borrowed beds.

34. (Kyorai)   Clouds over Tatara:
                 The sky still red.

35. (Bonchō)   Everywhere there
                 Harness-makers;
                 Cherry-flowers by the windows.

36. (Fumikuni) Through the medlar's old leaves
                 New buds begin to shoot.

CHIKAMATSU MONZAEMON

from *The Love Suicides at Sonezaki*

NARRATOR: To this world, farewell.
             To the night, too, farewell.
             He who goes to his death
             Is as the frost on the path
             To the burial ground,
             With every step melting away.
             This dream of a dream is sad.
             Ah! count the chimes —
             Seven to mark the dawn
             And six have tolled;
             The one that remains,
             The last fading echo in this life,
             The bell that echoes
             Coming joy beyond extinction.
             Not to the bell alone,
             To grass, to trees,
             To the sky, too, farewell.
             They look up for the last time —
             The clouds, too are heedless;
             On the water's surface
             The Plough star reflected bright,
             The Wife and Husband stars
             In the River of Heaven.[65]

TOKUBEI: The Bridge of Umeda –
            Let us vow it be
            The Bridge of Magpies
            And for ever let us be,
            You and I, Wife and Husband stars.

NARRATOR: 'It shall be so,' she says,
            And clings close to him.
            Tears fall, shed by both –
            The river water must have risen!
            Beyond the river, upstairs
            In one of the tea-houses,
            At the height of their love-making,
            Before they go to sleep,
            In the lamplight, voices raised,
            The leaves and grass of talk
            Flourish rank on the good and ill
            Of the suicides this year.

TOKUBEI: The heart sorrows to hear it.
            But man's fortune is mysterious;
            Until yesterday, until today,
            We too spoke as if of others' grief.
            But from the dawn we too
            Shall enter the list of gossip,
            Our song sung by the world –
            Let them sing then, if they must.

NARRATOR: And now they hear the song:[66]
            'Why will you not
            Take me as your wife?
            You may think of me as
            One you can do without.'
            We may love, we may grieve,
            But fortune and the world
            Are not as we would have them.
            Every day it is so; until today
            Never was there a day, a night,

When my heart was at rest,
Tortured by a love I should not feel.
'Why, oh why, is it so?
Not for an instant can I forget.
Should you want to discard me
And go your way, I'll not allow it.
Lay your hands on me, kill me,
Then be off – only thus
Shall I leave you free.'
Thus she sobbed through her tears.

TOKUBEI: Alas! that they should sing
This of all songs,
This night of all nights.
The singer – who it is, I know not;
The listeners – we; like those of the song,
Who passed long ago, our loves the same.

NARRATOR: They cling to one another, and,
Not sparing of their sobs, they weep;
And, like all lovers before them,
Pray for just a while together.
But such is the way of summer's night,
Short as always, short as love.
Then the crow of the cock,
Hounding their life span.

TOKUBEI: Oh, sorrow! Before the light
Let us die in Tenjin Grove.[67]

NARRATOR: He leads her by the hand.
The midnight rooks of Umeda Dyke

TOKUBEI: Tomorrow will prey on our flesh.[68]

OHATSU: Sad indeed that this year
Is thus for both ill-starred –
Twenty-five for you, for me nineteen;[69]
A token of our close-linked fates,
That loves and stars should be as one.

My vows to Spirits[70] and the Buddha,
Said for this life, now
I say for the life to come –
That in the world beyond
We may share a single lotus.[71]

NARRATOR: Nine twelves the beads
Of her rosary, rubbed and told;
And at their side a greater score
Of her jewel tear-drops.
Nine twelves the worldly lusts,
Passions, sorrows never spent,
But this world's journey done.
From their hearts, a black shade
In the sky; the wind dies out.
They come to their goal
In Sonezaki Grove.
There or here? They clear the grass,
Damp with the dew already fallen,
Dew that dies sooner than they.

SIXTY SENRYŪ

Now the man has a child
He knows all the names
Of the local dogs.

'My present mother
Is from the Yoshiwara,'[72]
He says.

Back from the festival
With the kids he took,
And dealing them out.

Zen priest,
Meditation finished,
Looking for fleas.

When it's of his wife
A fellow's afraid,
The money rolls in.

Not a single word
She says, and the house
Becomes the wife's.

Patching up a row,
It returns to normal:
The wife's voice.

In the beautiful woman,
Somewhere or other
His wife finds flaws.

She suckles her baby:
'On the shelf
You'll find some sardines.'

After he's scolded
His wife too much,
He cooks the rice.

In the whole village
The husband alone
Does not know of it.

Making it up –
To be the first to smile
Ashamed, it seems.

Rubbing her beads
So they click and rustle,
And finding fault.[73]

If it's well styled
There are stories about her –
The widow's hair.

Asked 'Did you hear it?'
'Have you eaten it?' –
He replied.[74]

Flung up at the moon,
Thrown down at the grass –
The dancer's hands.

Opening the door –
'Oh! oh! oh!'
Snow morning.

Sheltering from the rain,
The words on the notice
Are learnt off pat.

A horse farts:
Four or five suffer
On the ferry-boat.

Treading mid-river
In straw sandals,
The raft-master.

The one who's asleep
Was the very first
To call for his medicine.

As he enters the house,
A whiff of murder –
The quack-doctor.

'We can't all be the same' –
And the flower-viewing
Party splits up.[75]

The laundryman –
By his neighbours'
Grubbiness he lives.

The picture that
The guide can't read –
He doesn't show them that.

'She may have only one eye
But it's a pretty one,'
Says the go-between.

With his apology
For wings, as best he can
The duck flies.

At all the corners
The mat-maker
Curses the carpenter.

The morning after she's gone
He's very busy
Just finding everything.

The ladder-seller
Hears the cry 'Swords drawn!'
And scrambles to the roof.

The younger sister
First ferrets out
The groom's bad habits.

The whole village
Left more stylish
By the travelling troupe.

The number two priest
Looks as though he could do
With a puff or two.[76]

The bachelor
Gives humblest thanks
For a single stitch.

His loss known
To the whole world –
The china-shop.

If it could be wrapped
Water would make a fine
Present from Kyōto.

The prostitute, too,
When the game is slow
Changes her name.

Judging from the pictures,
Hell looks the more
Interesting place.

The *Nō* flute –[77]
Played as if it were
Forgotten for long stretches.

Discovered in the act,
The man stealing a horse
Mounts and rides away.

Setting out on a journey,
'Good-bye' the second time
Said with his sedge-hat.

The maid's letter –
Written as if in
Twisty Sanskrit characters.

His *magnum opus* –
While the wife does
The neighbours' sewing.

The fingerless nun:[78]
You smile at her
But she only smiles.

Making out she doesn't know
When she knows: when asked,
She says, 'I've no idea.' [79]

Guns blazing
From his fan,
The story-teller.

'I delivered
A bonny widow' –
His fellow-doctor.

Showing it to the locum –
What's the use
With a fool like that?

Till the laughter dies down,
On the dais
Mopping at his sweat.

Disturbed, the cat
Lifts its belly
On to its back.

The chicken wants
To say something –
Fidgeting its feet.

A letter from a man
She doesn't much care for –
Showing it to mother.

Not going in,
But asking the price,
Sheltering from the rain.

Letting rip a fart –
It doesn't make you laugh
When you live alone.

Getting out of bed
For a pee, the wife
Curses the chessmen.

Glaring glumly at the sky,
Pecking at their packed lunch
At home.

To the go-between
She says in a low voice,
'Delay it four or five days.'

When her daughter
Tightens her belly-band,
Mother's tension slackens.

His own face
He shines daily,
The mirror-polisher.

As it's such a sweat,
He cooks a whole gallon –
The bachelor.

KYŌKA

A blind-drunk
New Year caller
I see: spring
Coming, lurching
Across the street.
                    [by Shokusanjin]

The *haiku* monkey's
Straw raincoat, even –
Nowadays it seems
To want its *kyōka* clothes![80]
                    [by Shokusanjin]

Our poets had best
Be rather weak:
If heaven and earth
Began to move –
What a terrible mess![81]
                    [by Yadoya Meshimori]

Sweat dripping down
As you drill away at
The arts of the sword:
That they're no use,
May this reign be praised.

[by Moto Mokuami]

RYŌKAN

The hare in the moon

Long long ago, they say,
Lived a monkey, a hare, and a fox.
Together they formed a bond
Of friendship:
In the day, they romped
In the hills and fields,
At night, to their
Forest they returned.
And so time passed,
Until the god who lives
In the eternal heavens
Heard the story.
'But is it true?'
He asked, and turned himself
Into an old man,
Teetering along to see.
There he found them
Just as he had heard,
Romping and playing,
Their hearts made one.
Resting his limbs awhile,
Pausing to get his breath,
He threw away his staff
And shouted, 'Help me!

Help a hungry old man!'
'That's not hard,' they said,
And then, quick as a flash,
From the copse behind
The monkey gathered berries;
From the river bank in front
The fox snapped up a fish;
But the hare, hopping
All about the place,
Did not a thing to help.
'Oh! that hare – his idea's
Always different,' they cursed.
But all to no good. Then,
'Break these twigs,' said monkey,
'Light a fire,' said fox.
Hare did as he was told.
And then, into the smoke
And flames they hurled him,
And served him up to
The old man, all unwitting.
He, lifting his eyes
To the heavens that last for ever,
Sobbed and wept and then
Rolled prostrate on the ground.
Soon, beating on his breast,
He asked, 'Which of the three,
These three old friends, which
Treated me the best?
They were all kind.' And yet,
Thinking that the hare
Was the finest of them all,
He took him, dead,
And cast him high up
To the palace of the moon
In the heavens that last for ever.[82]

Even till today
This story has been told,
How the hare came
To live up in the moon.
And we, too, as we hear,
Dampen with our tears
The white hemp of our sleeves.

In the village,
Flute and drum
Are sounding.
Here on the hill,
The murmur of many pines.

In my begging bowl
Violets and dandelions
Are mixed together:
To the Buddhas of the Three Worlds[83]
I shall offer them.

Water I will draw,
Firewood I will cut,
Vegetables I will pick,
In the space before
Autumn's showers fall.

The wind is gentle,
The moon is bright.
Come then, together
We'll dance the night out
As a token of old age.

TACHIBANA AKEMI

Poems of solitary delights

What a delight it is
When on the bamboo matting
In my grass-thatched hut,
All on my own,
I make myself at ease.

What a delight it is
When, borrowing
Rare writings from a friend,
I open out
The first sheet.

What a delight it is
When, spreading paper,
I take my brush
And find my hand
Better than I thought.

What a delight it is
When, after a hundred days
Of racking my brains,
That verse that wouldn't come
Suddenly turns out well.

What a delight it is
When, of a morning,
I get up and go out
To find in full bloom a flower
That yesterday was not there.

What a delight it is
When, skimming through the pages
Of a book, I discover
A man written of there
Who is just like me.

What a delight it is
When everyone admits
It's a very difficult book,
And I understand it
With no trouble at all.

What a delight it is
When I blow away the ash,
To watch the crimson
Of the glowing fire
And hear the water boil.

What a delight it is
When a guest you cannot stand
Arrives, then says to you
'I'm afraid I can't stay long,'
And soon goes home.

What a delight it is
When I find a good brush,
Steep it hard in water,
Lick it on my tongue
And give it its first try.

FOLK-SONG

Lullabies

Than mind a child
That yelps like this
The rice-field weeds
I hate so much
I'd rather gather.

Than mind a child
That yelps like this
I'd all day work
The loom that creaks
Noisy as crickets.

'Is she sound asleep?' –
This I asked the pillow.
The pillow said, 'Yes, yes,
She's fallen fast asleep.'

Sleep, little one, sleep.
Why are his ears so long,
Baby rabbit of Sleepy Hill?
When his mother carried him
She ate acorns, mulberries.
That is why his ears
Have grown so very long.

Sleep, baby, sleep:
Sweet baby, go to sleep.
Too sweet for words, how could you tell
How sweet my baby is –
More than the trees on every hill,
More than every blade of grass,
More than all the stars in the sky,

More than the rice stalks in the field?
This babe asleep
Is more, more sweet
Than all of these.

Go to sleep, my baby,
Sleep, sleep, sleep.
My little babe,
When was she born?
In the third month
When cherries flower.
That's why her face
Is cherry pink.

[from Musashi]

Where has the guardian of sleep gone?
She went home across that hill.
What did she bring as presents from her home?
A drum to go 'brmm, brmm',
A tiny piping flute,
A tumbler-doll that always stands upright[84]
And a finger drum to shake and wave.
I'll bang the drum just once,
Then off to sleep, to sleep you go.
Sleep, sleep, fast asleep you go.

[from Aichi]

You, orphan child,
Bow to the setting sun:
For there your parents are –
In the sun as she sets.

[from Mie]

Children's songs

Huge snowflakes dancing down,
Great hailstones spattering.
At the back door
Dumplings are boiling,
Red beans are seething.
The hunter is returning,
The baby is howling,
And I can't find the ladle –
What a life, what a life!
                    [from Shimane]

Bracken fern,
Why are you so bent?

Because I grow along the ground,
That's why I'm so bent.

Then go and plant the paddy.

But if I plant the paddy
I'll become all muddied.

If you are all muddied,
Go and get a wash.

If I have a wash
Then I'll freeze to death.

If you're freezing cold,
Draw up to the fire.

If I warm myself,
I'll find I get too hot.

If you get too hot,
Have a lovely stretch.

If I stretch myself
I'll go hollow in my middle.

If you go all hollow
Find yourself a prop.

I find a prop
It's sure to make me hurt.

Oh well, if it hurts
It won't do any harm.

[from Hyōgo]

Hare, Mr Hare,
What is it that makes you hop?
I see the moon of the fifteenth night
And then I hop
Hoppety hoppety
Hop hop hop.

'I'm off to Kuwana Town,' old Pussy said.
On the Kuwana Road his torch went out –
He tried to light it but it wouldn't catch.
He sat his weary limbs on a tea-shop bench
And asked, 'Won't you give me just a drink of water?'
'It's easy enough to give you water, but
The bottom of the bucket's just dropped off.'
Oh dear, what a mean old hag!
'Then just a tiny swig of tea?'
'It's easy enough to make you tea, but
The bottom of the kettle's just dropped off.'
Oh dear, what a mean old hag!
'Then how about a whiff of shag?'
'It's easy enough to give you shag, but
The bowl of my pipe has just dropped off.'
Oh dear, what a mean old hag!
One, two, three, four, five, six,
Seven, eight, nine, T-E-N.

[from Shimane]

Oi! oi! Firefly, here!
The water there's all bitter,
The water here's so sweet!
Oi! oi! Firefly, here!

[from Kantō]

Paddy snail, paddy snail,
Off you go to the hills.
'I went there in the spring last year
And a great black bird that's called a crow
Pecked me on this side and turned me on my back,
Pecked me on that side and turned me on my back.
No! Never a second time for me, going to those hills!'

[from Nagano]

Counting-song

Just listen to the grumbles of
The nursemaid of Niigata.
First: at four she's up and dressed.[85]
Two: takes the baby on her back:
Three: thwacked: four, flayed with words.
Five: filthy plates and pans to clean.
Six: sick and tired of rotten food.
Seven: smelly nappies all to wash.
Eight: aching, sore, and shedding tears.
Nine: nerves and bones all worked to death.
Ten: tasked by master, 'How are things?'
Her mouth won't open, like a putrid walnut.

[from Niigata]

Lyrics of the Bon *Dance*

Bon, the sixteenth night –
I've waited since New Year.
Sixteenth night, I've waited long,
Tonight, tonight alone.

[from Iwate]

Whether you dance or don't
It's tonight or never.
For from tomorrow it's
Rice-mowing in the paddies.

[from Akita]

It's *Bon*, it's *Bon* – but
Only today and tomorrow.
The next day we're up in the hills
Cutting grass for fodder.

[from Chiba]

If my man were a beggar
How much better it would be.
None would then get stuck on him
And he'd be left for me.

[from Niigata]

It's *Bon*, it's *Bon*, so beat the drum and sing.
Today's the sixteenth day of *Bon*:
Tomorrow up the hills we go,
To cut the drooping grass,
To cut the drooping grass
So fast my sickle handle's broke.
Still, what matter that it's broke:
Aren't there smithies in this land?
Yes, six smithies in this land.
We'll go and sing all six our song.

[from Aichi]

'Are you dancing in the *Bon*?'
'Yes – because this year
There's no babe in my belly
And I feel light as air.'

           [from Wakayama]

'Why don't you girls over there come along tonight?
Don't you have a drum and a bamboo whisk?'

'Oh, they're all ready, drum and bamboo whisk,
But we've also got a seven-month child in here.'

'Oh, seven months, eight months, hide it with your sleeve:
It's when it comes to ten months you'll find it hard to hide.'

           [from Tokyo]

Anyone not tempted out
By the red loincloths of *Bon*
Is a Buddha made of wood or bronze,
A Buddha made of stone.

           [from Mie]

If you dance this dance,
Better dance it well.
Those who dance it best
They say
Are better bets for brides.

           [raditional]

We promised to see
The moon come up.
The moon came up early.
The forest was dark.

           [from Fukushima]

Handsome boy!
O for a thread
To haul him over
To my side!

[from Fukushima]

When I was young,
Hands pulled at my skirt.
Now children and grandchildren
Tug at my hands.

[from Fukushima]

Rice-planting songs

Oh! my hips hurt so!
My shoulders ache!
Where can I give my legs a rest?
I know! I'll move Amida Buddha
And lie down at his side.

[from Aomori]

At sundown the little birds
Rustle in the bushes.
But I – I nestle in the breasts
Of a girl who plants the rice.

[from Kyōto]

O for a babe still at the breast
In the month of May:
Then I'd feed him once or twice
And rest my weary waist.

[from Fukuoka]

In the paddy grow the weeds,
In dry fields grow the tares:
At night I get my oats
And wear my strength away.
          [from Shizuoka]

At *Bon* we dance,
At New Year, sleep,
All day in June
Keep picking weeds.
          [from Kyōto]

The scarecrow doesn't worry him,
The rattle doesn't startle him,
In the autumn fields so bare, so bare
A lonely bird pecks rice.
          [from Fukushima]

When spring comes,
There's water in the paddy pools.
The mudloach and the singing frog
Are happy, are happy,
Thinking they're in the sea.

When summer comes,
The paddy pools grow warm.
The mudloach and the singing frog
Are happy, are happy,
Thinking they're in a bath.

When autumn comes,
The hills and dales turn red.
The mudloach and the singing frog,
Craning their necks above,
Must think the hills on fire.

When winter comes,
The paddy pools are filmed with ice.
The mudloach and the singing frog
Must think their heaven has stretched,
Has stretched and grown above.

[from Aomori]

Miscellaneous

Mogami's tea-house –
Where I left that umbrella.
Whenever it rains
I remember it all.

[from Miyagi]

That hill is too high
To see Shinjō.[86]
Shinjō: my love.
Hill: my hate.

[from Yamagata]

I, too, in my day
Was bidden, 'Come.'
Today, like rain in autumn,
No use to anyone.

[from Iwate]

My arms didn't clasp
My lassie's waist.
It was a tree
My arms embraced,
And the tree didn't say a word.

[Mountain song from Aomori]

Modern Period

(from 1868)

1. *Tanka*
2. *Haiku*
3. Modern *Senryū*
4. *Shintaishi ('New-Style Poetry')*

1. *Tanka*

EMPEROR MEIJI

In my garden
Side by side
Native plants, foreign plants,
Growing together.

The young go off
To the gardens of battle.
Old men alone
Guard our fields at home.

Whenever I see
The writings of the past,
I ponder: 'How are
The people I rule?'

'For ever and ever
Protect my people,
Guard my reign': thus I pray
To the great Gods of Ise.

In newspapers, all see
The doings of the world,
Which lead nowhere:
Better never written!

ITŌ SACHIO

When cowherds begin
To make poems,
Many new styles
In the world
Will spring up.

Standing there,
This morning's cold
Startled me!
Soft dew: piled deep,
Fallen persimmon leaves.

I have forsaken
The land of men,
And have come to a place
Where white waves
Split earth in two.

No high mountains,
No lowly hills:
At the earth's limits
Before my eyes
The heavens fall.

Beyond the back door
Nothing to see.
Cold, chilling:
Clouded sun leaning
On withered reeds.

MASAOKA SHIKI

Village snuffed asleep,
Lights all gone out,
Stars silvery white
Over the bamboo clump.

I thought to make
A trellis for the moonflower.
Ah! My life can
Hardly last till autumn.

YOSANO AKIKO

You never touch
This soft skin
Surging with hot blood.
Are you not bored,
Expounding the Way?

Spring is short:
Why ever should it
Be thought immortal?
I grope for
My full breasts with my hands.

The sutra is sour:
This spring evening,
O Twenty-Five Saints[87]
Of the inner sanctuary,
Accept my songs instead.

No camellia
Nor plum for me,

No flower that is white.
Peach blossom has a colour
That does not ask my sins.

SAITŌ MOKICHI

On the mountain
Where the silver
Snow is falling
Is a narrow path
Where men pass.

Close to death
Lying next to mother:
The raucous croak
Of paddy frogs
Reaches the heavens.

Faded vine flowers
Fluttering down
On the mountainside:
The call of the dove
So forlorn.

Crimson tomato
Rotten to the core:
My footsteps, too,
Not far away
From such a state.

The light pink
Of the cat's tongue:
My hand touches and
I begin to know
This misery.

WAKAYAMA BOKUSUI

How forlorn
Is the white bird!
Sky and sea both
Blue: yet untinged
He hovers there.

Like a bubbling stream,
The call of the bird
From among the pines
And the mountain cherries:
Mountain-fold, noon.

The hill asleep:
At its feet
The sea asleep:
Through forlorn spring
I travel on.

On the sea-bed
Eyeless fish live,
So they say:
That I might be
Such eyeless fish!

At my side
Autumn weed-flowers
Whisper softly –
'How dear to me
Are all things that die.'

ISHIKAWA TAKUBOKU

Weeping, sobbing
On a beach of white sand
On an Eastern Sea island,
Flirting with the crabs.

Carrying mother on my back
Just for a joke.
Three steps: then weeping –
She's so light.

Working, working.
Yet no joy in life,
Still staring emptily
At empty hands.

A day when I yearn for home
As if I were ill:
Gloom of the smoky sky.

In the crowd at the station
I heard words they use at home.
O to go back . . .

They might have hurled stones
To drive me out.
Memory that can never be dulled.

On the far river bank
Fresh green, the tender willow:
As if she said, 'Weep for me.'

In the snow
Softly drifting,
Hot cheeks buried:
Love, for me.

Today, my friends seemed
More a success than I.
So I bought flowers
And took them to
My wife, to make her happy.

In a single night
The storm-wind came
And built high up
This mound of sand.
Whose grave is it?

I write in the sand
The word 'great'
More than a hundred times.
Then I go back home,
Dropping all thought of death.

Through the train window,
Far away to the north,
The hills above my home
Come slowly into sight,
And I straighten my collar.

The wind in the pines
Soughs night and day
In the ears of the stone horse
At a mountain shrine
Where no man worships.

2. *Haiku*

NAITŌ MEISETSU

Early winter:
Bamboos green
At Shisendō.[88]

The wind blows grey,
The sun sets through
The winter copse.

Clods of earth
Seeming to move?
No – quail.

Hill field: under the moon
Someone still ploughing
Above Mama Village.[89]

MASAOKA SHIKI

Looking through
Three thousand *haiku*
On two persimmons.

A snake falls
From the high stone wall:
Fierce autumn gale.

He washes his horse
With the setting sun
In the autumn sea.

Again and again
From my sickbed I ask,
'How deep is the snow?'

Soon to die,
Yet noisier than ever:
The autumn cicada.

Snake-gourd in bloom:[90]
On his way to death,
A man choked with phlegm.

A crimson berry
Splattering down on
The frost-white garden.

As the bat flies,
Its sound is dark
Through the grove of trees.

I want to sleep:
Go gently, won't you,
When you swat the flies.

So few the cicadas
This morning after
The autumn storm.

KAWAHIGASHI HEKIGOTŌ

Cold spring day:
Above the fields
Rootless clouds.

The *Nō* by torchlight:
On the woman's mask
One shaft of light.[91]

TAKAHAMA KYOSHI

Autumn wind:
Everything I see
Is *haiku*.

The snake fled,
But the eyes that watched
Still in the grass.

On the stolen
Scarecrow's hat,
Sudden shower.

On far hills
The sun catches:
Bleak moorland.

Against the broad sky
Stretching and leaning,
Winter trees.

Shuttlecock:
Smooth as oil
The words of Kyōto.[92]

The sky is high:
The tips of tendrils
Have nowhere to cling.

In the old man's eyes
The piercing sun
Looks fuddled.

Like dust swirling
At the height of winter,
News of his death.

First butterfly –
Like a dream
Lost to sight.

Even sparrows
Freed from all fear of man
England in spring.[93]

WATANABE SUIHA

Waves on the ebb,
Sound fading away:
Autumn evening.

The noisy cricket
Soaks up the moonbeams
On the wet lawn.

Wild geese flying
In stiff, stiff lines –
The sky colder.

Autumn wind:
Eyes distended,
Red cicada shrieks.[94]

IIDA DAKOTSU

Above her sash,
Breasts in her way
As she tucks in her fan.

Iron autumn
And all the cold
Windbells tinkling.

Udders dripping,
The cow lumbers by:
Autumn day.

Dragging across
Snow-covered mountains,
The echo goes.

In the winter lamp,
Dead face not far
From the living face.

HARA SEKITEI

Warm and snug,
Ageing in his sleep,
The paddy snail.

Feeling lonely
He strikes the gong again,
Guard of the hill-paddy.

Stepping on a tendril,
A whole hill of dew
Begins to move.

The autumn storm dying,
Here and there, slowly,
Men's voices come to life.

On scattered hailstones
The grasses' shadows:
The sun is savage.

MIZUHARA SHŪŌSHI

Pear blossoms:
Over Katsushika Plain[95]
Mild, misted sky.

Stars above the peaks;
Silkworm hamlet
Fast asleep.[96]

Gathering water-oats,
The boy half asleep
Rowing his boat.

The reed-warbler –
Its song pierces
Grey morning mist.

Everywhere, everywhere,
Fields and rape-seed
Flashing in confusion.

KAWABATA BŌSHA

On the snow
Alighting gently,
The nightingale.

Bright moonlight:
The wounds in the deep snow
Will not be hidden.

Nothing there but
The whorl of a fern:
This floating world.

Hearing the thunder-clap
As if it struck my lungs:
Yet still alive.

Wasting in summer:
Arms heavier
Than iron bars.

Pillow hard as stone!
Am I a cicada
That I scream so loud?

NAKAMURA KUSADAO

Undergraduates,
By and large shabby:
Wild geese flying off.[97]

Already winter:
An old tombstone
Taken for a signpost.

A father at last –
Like a lizard,
Stopping, starting, stopping.

Family reunion:
Evening cicadas
Starting up in the trees.

Gentle as my dead friend's hand
Resting on my shoulder,
This autumn sunshine.

KATŌ SHŪSON

Sad and forlorn: the shrike
Bears on its back
The gold of the sunset.

Sticking out my head from
The hot hell of the mosquito net –
Autumn wind.

Autumn wind –
I open out
My ashen palm.

MATSUMOTO TAKASHI

Her summer *kimono*
Loose, untied,
Yet somehow trim.

Cicadas shrieking:
The arc of stars
Grows steeper still.

In the brothel
A room, empty:
Autumn evening.

On an onion tuft
A butterfly settling:
Lonely, sad.

ISHIDA HAKYŌ

Sparrows scurrying
As if storm-mounted
Scudding over fields.

Sick-room window
Lacquered over
With grey winter cloud.

Dead fly husk
Lies by my sleeve
As if in waiting.

3. Modern *Senryū*

At the shouts and cheers
The grandstand seems
Just about to collapse.

So hard to fall for –
The female
English-language typist.

The carp pennant[98]
Bellying in the wind,
Fuji looks the lower.

Now she's got a baby,
Even her piano
Gives no satisfaction.

Now she's borne her brat
She brazenly lays bare
Her buxom breasts.

The tram-car full,
'Stop shoving,' they shout,
And go on shoving.

The accent back home –
The more you hide it
The broader it gets.

As bad as a dyer's –
Finger-tips stained
From pickling plums.

Making her doll
Play younger sister –
The only child.

A doll as well
On top of the clothes-chest
In the newly-weds' house.

Every Sunday
Learning the facts of life –
The young soldier.

In the child's homework
A word he doesn't know –
Father's face.

Handing back the baby,
The wet-nurse finds
Her lap feels empty.

Masked by the pines
By his mistress's house,
He forgoes the bowing.

In the policeman's arms
The lost child points
Towards the sweet-shop.

'Keep left! To the left!'
The constable waving
His right arm instead.

On the pilgrimage to Ise,[99]
Swapping notes on
How many grandchildren.

Losing in love,
His feet crumble under him,
Sodden with gin.

When she wails
At the top of her voice,
The husband gives in.

The traveller in bed,
Turning and turning,
Trying to get off.

Found while spring-cleaning
But too precious to throw out,
The first love's letters.

All its advertisements
Given over to the wind –
The windbell shop.

While she ties her sash,
He waits at her side,
Cheeks held in palms.

The winter fly
Weakly collides
With the sliding doors.

Going down in
The lift, it gives
A gloomy feeling.

Outlandish names
For local food
Sold at the station.

A famous horse,
Now, in the zoo,
Forgotten.

Sheltering from rain,
By the empty tea-shop's
Bugs bitten.

The father of the son
On his Grand Tour
Has gone quite bald.

Waiting for his turn
For the European trip,
The D. Litt., ageing.

European food –
Every blasted plate
Is round.

The medicine-fetcher
Trudges through snow
Down silent streets.

Water mirror:
Making you suspect
Your own face a bit.

4. *Shintaishi ('New-Style Poetry')*

TSUCHII BANSUI

Moon over the ruined castle

Spring in its tall towers, flower-viewing banquets,
The wine-cup passed and glinting in the light
Streaming through pine branches a thousand ages:
That moonlight of the past – where is it now?

Autumn: the white hoarfrost across the camp,
Counting the wild geese, crying as they flew:
Light of the past flashing on row on row
Of planted swords: that light – where is it now?

Now, over the ruined castle the midnight moon,
Its light unchanged; for whom does it shine?
In the hedge, only the laurel is left behind:
In the pines, only the wind of the storm still sings.

High in the heavens the light remains unchanged.
Glory and decay are the mark of this shifting earth.
Is it to copy them now, brighter yet,
Over the ruined castle the midnight moon?

SHIMAZAKI TŌSON

By the old castle at Komoro

By the old castle at Komoro
The clouds are white and the wanderer grieves.
The green chickweed does not sprout

And the young grass is too thin for carpet.
The silver quilt covering the hills
Melts in the sun to make a stream of shallow snow.

The light of the sun is warm
But the scent does not fill the fields;
Spring is only shallow, hazed.
The colour of the corn is a wan green.
Some bands of travellers
Hurry along the path through the fields.

It grows dark, Asama disappears:
Sound of a reed flute, its note plaintive.
The waves of Chikuma River falter.
I put up in an inn near its bank
And drink, fuddled by *sake* dregs,
And, grass for pillow, rest on my journeying.

Song of travel on the Chikuma River

Yesterday again it was so,
Today too again it will be so.
Why do we fuss and fret in this life,
Anxious always for tomorrow?

Often I have gone down into the valley
Where the dream lingers of growth and decline,
And seen the hesitant river waves,
Sand-filled water coil and return.

Ah! The old castle – what does it say?
The ripples by the bank – what do they reply?
Think silently on the age that has gone,
A hundred years even as yesterday.

The willows of Chikuma River grow dim:
A shallow spring, water drifting away.
Alone, I wander among the rocks,
And to this bank I tie my cares.

Coconut

From a far-off island whose name I do not know
A coconut is swept in.

Separated from your native shore
How many months have you been on the waves?

Is the old tree still alive, still flourishing?
Are its branches still shady?

I pillow my head again by the sea,
A lone, floating wanderer.

I take the coconut and hold it to my heart:
The grief of the wanderer is renewed.

Tears welling up in a strange land,
I watch the sun set in the sea.

Endlessly moving tide, feeling with me,
Will I ever return to my home?

KAMBARA ARIAKE

Oyster shell

The oyster in his oyster shell,
In the sea, limitless,
Alone, in danger, confined,
His thoughts so sad.

Blind and artless,
He sleeps in rock shade,
But when he wakes he feels
The ebb and flow of tides.

At morning tide, at black dawn –
However bathed in light, in clearness –
The oyster's body, which must shrivel,
Stays locked in its shell.

The evening star, however clear
Its light, flashing on crests of waves,
May seem like the image of a dove
In a far field. But not to him.

Yes, it is sad. The wonder
Of the deep burden of the ocean
Night and day, unbearable:
In affliction, he shuts his shell.

Yet once the storm blows up,
On the day when sea-forests are uprooted,
The oyster's body which must shrivel,
How can it not be smashed?

TAKAMURA KŌTARŌ

Bedraggled ostrich

What fun to keep an ostrich!
In its thirty-odd square feet of mud at the zoo,
Aren't its legs too straddling?
Isn't its neck too long?
In a land where snow falls, wouldn't its feathers get bedraggled?
Famished, no doubt it would gobble up even hard tack.
But aren't ostrich's eyes for ever looking only into the distance?
They blaze as if body and world were non-existent.
Isn't it waiting desperately for an emerald wind to blow?
Isn't it infinite dreams that twist back that puny, artless head?
Isn't it no longer an ostrich –
More a *man*?

Oh, pack it in! That sort of talk gets you nowhere.

Artless talk

'There is no sky in Tokyo,' Chieko said:
She longed to see the true sky.

Startled, I looked at the sky.

Through the young cherry leaves
Stretched a sky, infinite, tasting of the past.
The horizon's leaden gloom was tinted
With morning's sliver of damp pink.

Gazing through the distant haze,
Chieko spoke of the blue sky hanging
Each day over the hill at home.

That is Chieko's true sky:
Artless talk of an artless sky.

Chieko mounting on the wind

Crazed Chieko no longer utters words;
Only making signs to the blue magpie and the plover.
Over the line of wind-break mounds
Pine-pollen spreads, yellow.
In the clear May wind, the beach is dim;
Chieko's gown – now hidden among the pines, now appearing.
On the white sand mushrooms grow.
I pick mushrooms as I
Slowly follow Chieko.
Blue magpie and plover are Chieko's companions,
Chieko, now no longer woman.
Dazzling morning sky her favourite playground
Where Chieko flies.

KITAHARA HAKUSHŪ

Rain on Castle Island

Rain:
Grey, rat-grey rain
On Castle Island shore;

Rain:
Is it pearls or
Evening mist, or my tears?

A boat
Puts out – my man's
Boat, sail and mast dripping.

Boats
Moved by oars; oars
By songs; songs by the bos'n's mood.

Rain
From cloud-grey sky.
Boat bobbing, sail distant, dim.

Larches

Through the larch forest,
Turning to look back.
Lonely larches,
Lonely journey.

Through the larch forest
Into the next,
A narrow path
Going through forests.

The road I take leads
To the heart of the larch forest:
Hill mist on the path,
Path swept by hill wind.

Do I go alone
Down the path through the larch forest?
The path is narrow, lonely:
I quicken my pace.

On through the larch forest
And stopping involuntarily:
Larch, lonely larch,
Whispering, breathing larch.

Through the larch forest
Smoke stands above Asama Peak.
Smoke stands above Asama Peak
Towering through the larch forest.

Rain falls in the larch forest,
Lonely rain, still rain.
Only the cuckoo calling,
Only the larches dripping.

The world is sorrow,
Inconstant, yet happy.
Only the hill stream gurgles,
Only the wind in the larches.

ISHIKAWA TAKUBOKU

After a fruitless argument

What we read and what we argue over
And the light in our eyes
Are not inferior to young Russians fifty years ago.
We argue what's to be done –
Yet, even so, not one of us clenches his fist,
Crashes it on the table
And shouts V NAROD.[100]

We know what it is we want:
We know what the people want
And we know what's to be done.
Yes, we know more than young Russians of fifty years ago.
Yet, even so, not one of us clenches his fist,
Crashes it on the table
And shouts V NAROD.

It is the young who are assembled here –
The young, always building something new for the world.
We knew the old would die before long and we should win.
Look at the light in our eyes, at the savagery of our arguments.
Yet even so, not one of us clenches his fist,
Crashes it on the table
And shouts V NAROD.

Fresh candles three times now:
Dead flies in our empty tea-cups:
The girls' zest unabated: yet
In their eyes the exhaustion at the end of a fruitless argument.
Yet even so, not one of us clenches his fist,
Crashes it on the table
And shouts V NAROD.

Rather than cry

It was in a dream –
What year, what night I do not remember –
That I met her.
She'll be dead and gone by now.

Heavy larding of oil on her black hair,
White as the fur of a rabbit dying in torment
Her thick powder,
Blood-coloured lipstick daubed on her mouth,

Among a crowd of girls she sang filthy songs
One after another, to a sprightly *samisen*.[101]
Putting down, as if it were water,

Stuff that took the skin off your tongue.
By her side, young sprouts
Of twenty, not drinking.

'Why sing like this?' I asked,
In my dream.
And she replied,
With a drunken, flushed laugh,
'Rather than cry . . .'

HAGIWARA SAKUTARŌ

Sick face at the base of the earth

At the base of the earth, a face:
A sick and lonely face.
In the gloom at the base of the earth
Grass stalks slowly starting to shoot,
A rat's nest beginning to sprout;
Tangled in the nest
Countless hairs quivering.
At the winter solstice,
From the sick, desolate earth
Slender bamboo roots sprouting green,
Starting to sprout.
So full of sadness,
So tender, so weak,
So full, full of sadness.

In the gloom at the base of the earth
A sick and lonely face.

The new Koide Highway

Here the newly opened highway
Leads straight into town.
From an intersection of the new highway
Horizon stretching endless, desolate in all directions
Murky day
Sun low under house eaves lining the highway
Trees in the grove felled here, felled there.
No! No! I shall not change my mind
I turn my back on the highway
All the young trees are felled.

Putrid clam

Part buried
Yet its tongue lolling out
Over the head of this clam
Shingle and sea water flowing *scrunch scrunch scrunch*
Flowing
Flowing calmly as in a dream.

From the gaps between flowing swirls of sand,
The clam again flickers, flickers its tongue, burning red
This clam is wasted away.
Its pulpy innards appear to be rotting
And so when sad evening comes
Settling on the sallow shore
It will flicker its rotten breath flicker flicker.

Cock

Before dawn
Cock crowing outside doorways
Long trembling call
Mother calling from the desolate countryside
Tō-te-kū   tō-ru-mō   tō-ru-mō.

In morning's chill bed
Fluttering of my soul's wings
In the gaps between these shutters
Everywhere the scenery sparkles
Yet before dawn
Gloom steals into my bed
Over misted treetops
Calling from the distant countryside, the cock's crow
Tō-te-kū   tō-ru-mō   tō-ru-mō.

My love
My love
In the shadow of daybreak's chill screens
Faint smell of chrysanthemums
Like the smell of a sick ghost
Faint smell of white chrysanthemums rotting
My love
My love.

Before dawn
My spirit wanders graveyard shadows
Ah, what is it? Heavy fretfulness calling me.

Unbearable pale red air
My love
Come quickly, put the light out
I hear the roar of a typhoon blowing through the earth's furthest
     ends
Tō-te-kū   tō-ru-mō   tō-ru-mō.

MIKI ROFŪ

Home

Back at my home,
Among the trees in the field
The notes of a flute:
Night — clouded moon.

The young girl
In her heart, burning,
Heard those notes:
Her tears flowed.

Ten years ago.
In that same heart
Do you weep, even
Though now a mother?

After the kiss

'Are you asleep?'
'No,' you say.

Flowers in May
Flowering at noon.

In the lakeside grass
Under the sun,
'I could close my eyes
And die here,' you say.

TSUBOI SHIGEJI

Autumn in gaol

In autumn a friend
Sent in an apple.
I made to eat it
All at once.
Red: too red.

In my palm, heavy:
Heavy as the world.

Star and dead leaves

A star was talking with the withered leaves
In the still midnight.
Only the wind stirred round me then.
Strangely forlorn,
I tried to share their words.

The star swooped from the heavens.

I searched among dead leaves
But could not ever find it.

English – ugh!

One morning, reading the paper, I was flabbergasted.
A well-known singer
On his way home on pay-day,
Was set on by hot-headed Fascists
In a bar
Because, a bit out of sorts,
He sang his favourite song in English.

What a suspicious world it is!
But how about
Those Fascists drinking
Un-Japanese beer? Interesting!

I read the report and thought:
If these bastards
Hate English all that much,
As revenge, and to test the skill of their thugs,
How would it be if, from end to end of Japan,
They set on, one by one,
All who speak English?

The immediate quarry would be the teacher of English.
Japan may well be narrow, but

She is a land where education booms;
There might be one, two, thousand teachers of English.
So, however mailed the Fascists' fists,
They'd have no end of trouble.

I remembered that
The Franco-Anglo-Japanese Girls' School in Kanda[102]
Had been renamed – the sweeter-scented Academy of the White
    Lily.
Before our 'State of Emergency', this girls' school
Went by its first name, with
France at the head,
England for its body
And Japan, the vital part,
Down at the feet. Scandalous! Insult!
So, when all was said and done, it had to be
The Girls' Academy of the White Lily.
Well! By such penman's logic
What on earth happens to dictionary names?
'Japanese-English dictionary' may pass,
But how about 'English-Japanese dictionary'?
Bloody English
French
German
Russian
Any foreign language!
Get out of Japan right now!
Then
Our Fascists can be at ease
And take their time over their beer in bars,
Getting tight,
Uninterrupted by songs in English,
Bellowing out our own songs.

Who is he?
– The bastard who keeps yarping that 'bar' is English?
Isn't there a worthy Japanese word for it? –
Sake-spot.

And the beer they're drinking?
That is barley-brew.
Or, rather, wheat-wine to our Fascist friends.

Butterfly

In the sample room
My dead body laid in place
With a line of others like me,
Pierced with a pin:
Quiet, like a mourning-band.

Yet the gaunt angular entomologist
Bends his head and broods.
Now and then my wings
Quiver a little.

'Ah – this one's not quite dead yet,
Cheeky little thing!
Or was it the wind?'
So the entomologist slammed the window.

Yes: I know I'm no longer alive,
Just a specimen butterfly. Yet
If the window's closed so tight
I'll suffocate to death.

Disturbed by my delirious talk,
My wife got out of bed
And softly opened the window.

Outside, like flowers bursting into bloom,
The night was bright:
So bright that it brought tears.

Silent, but . . .

I may be silent, but
I'm thinking.
I may not talk, but
Don't mistake me for a wall.

HORIGUCHI DAIGAKU

Landscape

Curves of a woman's body,
Swelling, undulating, tangled:
The triangle of a sun-baked island floating
In a beautiful soft sea of milk.
Lacklustre ferns growing luxuriantly:
Gentle curves flowing plumply in three undulations
Across the heart of the island. At the nub,
In the shadows of the trees grown rank in the valley,
The tapered roof of the headman's house, now here, now out of
    sight;
Peach-pink tapering house, now here, now out of sight.

Hammock

Hammock spread by a spider
And in it a butterfly rocks.

Shrouded in its golden halo
It dies.
   Like that butterfly
I, climbing to the hammock of your love
Rocking, would go to my death.
   Rocking.

Memories

Hordes of women wept for me;
Who was which I really don't recall.

Many faces all coming together
To make one, the face of a weeping girl,
Like a film, a dim vision
Through a boring day's tobacco haze,
A sentimental movie.

One lived in Mexico,
Mother of a boy the image of me.
Eyes dewed in tears of the past,
She would say to her boy,
'Your father died
Before you were born.'

One was a devout Spaniard,
Idolized by an old roué.
In her bedroom, Christ on the Cross,
Behind Christ, a picture of me.
She was devout; she never forgot
Her morning and evening prayers.

One would stare at the marks
Of my teeth on her milk-white skin.
That was how we did it then;
Still she thinks on and yearns for the past.

Another has an N tattooed
In the shadow of her breast.
When anyone curious asks,
'A keepsake of what?'
She laughs nervously and mutters
'Why should I remember?'

Hordes of women wept for me;
Who was which I really don't recall.

SAIJŌ YASO

The crow's letter

I opened and read
The small red envelope
The mountain crow had brought:
'On the night of the moon
The hills will blaze
Savage and red.'

I was going to reply,
When my eyes opened.
Ah yes, there it was:
A single red leaf.

SATŌ HARUO

Song of the pike

Ah
Autumn wind
If you have any compassion, go and tell her
That the man
For supper tonight, alone
Ate pike
And thought of her.

Pike, pike . . .
Squeeze the sour juice of a green tangerine over it
Then eat it – that is what they do at his home.
Curious, then attached to this habit,
Time after time she would pick a green tangerine ready for his
    supper.
Ah, a wife soon to be renounced by her husband and
A man deserted by his wife, facing across the supper table.[103]

A little girl, unloved by her father,
Struggling with her baby chopsticks.
'Give me that juicy bit,' she says to the man not her father.

Ah
Autumn wind
Take a good look
At this happy gathering not of this world.
Autumn wind, please
Bear witness that this happy gathering
Once was not a dream.

Ah
Autumn wind
If you have any compassion, go and tell
The wife who has not yet lost her husband
And the little girl who has not yet lost her father
That the man
For supper tonight, alone
Ate pike
And wept.

Pike, pike . . .
Are you bitter, are you salty?
Where is it that they eat pike
With warm tears squeezed over it?
Ah
Is my question really absurd?

TANAKA FUYUJI

Lakeside hotel

Lakeside hotel:
Gleam in August of young trout in a mountain tarn.

Mountain reflections, clear, tumbling into the tarn:
On my white shirt, the dull rouge glow
Of your silk parasol.
I casually pointing out the yachts on the tarn
To you – you so beautiful –
Asking you, 'Why is a boat feminine?'

You smiling faintly and not answering
And keeping to your talk of Hauptmann's *Sunken Bell*.
In the sunlight, seeping through white birch-leaves,
Your hair glints in the Southern Cross.

Autumn night

Chilly now: insects pestering round the lights.
I close the *shōji*[104] and
A face like a Taiping rebel's is reflected back, large.[105]
Settling down quietly, drinking sugared water,
I write till late.
My gown, put aside so long, smells of long ago.
Then, a lonely sound, again
A woman's cough from near the honey-locust.
I open the *shōji* to look, but not a soul; only
Like silver paper,
The still autumn night, all sound asleep.

Blue night road

The sky full of stars,
The blue night road
Seeming to lead to them,
The distant village
Bathed in some blue-green wine.

Tick tock tick
On his back in a cloth,
His clock repaired in the town,
The youth goes tick tock tick.

Lonely, as though he carried something living:
The stars, drowsy,
Pregnant with moisture, falling
In such numbers that they seem
To haunt the road to the white barns of the village.

NISHIWAKI JUNZABURŌ

Rain

With the south wind a gentle goddess came.
She soaked the bronze, she soaked the fountain,
She soaked the swallow's belly and its feathers of gold.
She hugged the tide, lapped the sand, drank the fish.
Secretly she soaked the temple, the bath-house, the theatre,
The confusion of her platinum lyre –
The tongue of the goddess – secretly
Soaked my tongue.

Weather

Morning like an upturned jewel:
A man murmuring with someone at the door –
Birthday of the gods.

Eye

White waves springing on my head, in July
I pass through a pretty southern town.
A quiet garden asleep to travellers
Roses, sand, water,
My heart misted by the roses
Hair incised on stone
Sounds incised on stone
Eyes, incised on stone, for ever open.

KANEKO MITSUHARU

Song of the tart

The very day the war ended
At the burnt-out, smoke-grimed street corners,
Unannounced, there you were –
I saw you, loafing and loitering.

You, your orang-outang hair dosed with drugs,
Your faces smeared thick with powder,
White as an enamelled chamber pot:
You rewrote your eyebrows and lips
On the model of the false mask of the Saipan shield.[106]

Where did you come from?
Or rather, through the long war, where
Did you hide yourselves?
And how could you change so swiftly?

Dangling on the arms of men, you
Rampage the streets of debris, where
Jazz is heard from below the tombs.
The direction you walk in . . .
As if you could call it a direction.

Everyone, shocked, watches you,
Eyes turned as you pass;
Eyes that are nervous,
Absent-minded, abstracted.

You, distorted, only half there, gross,
An almost brutal joke: but so sudden to me
That it is beyond any joke.
All I wish is to be shocked,
Then to shock you.

To silence all – half-hearted humanism
And literature, fussy, fidgety politics,
Smart theories – silence every one of them.

God! look! There they are again,
A bunch of them by the station,
Swarming under the smashed street lamps.
Are they *Nō* masks – the weeping old man
And *Mikenjaku* – that look at me?[107]

Knees pressed into shoes, tubs, mortars –
That's the feeling you give me,
You, your gory lips
Puffing Chesterfields,
Cudding chewing gum.

Gaping yawn from a tart,
A red O,
And in the O, black gloom,
Flesh-red gloom.

Freckled yellow skin,
Grazed knees:
Men turn round,
She catches eyes, sleeves.

She yawns, fit
To swallow a man whole.
Never in Japan a crater
As gaping as this yawn.

Wordy, tedious debates,
War guilt, liberalism,
All these flung into the abyss
Of that tart's yawn
Make only a ripple.

Ascension

Today is execution day for the pacifists.
Escaping from the gunfire as their corpses topple,
Their souls have ascended to heaven.
To proclaim injustice and iniquity.

In grief, their spirits have begun to relent,
Calling from the edge
Of a great four-cornered ice-floe,
Turning to a rainbow flickering in the dark.

Bombs have exploded; fireworks have crackled:
Their souls, sent drifting to one corner of heaven,
Turned into mist, into spume, into cloud-drifts,
To stain the sky with blood that is still hot.

Opposition

In my youth
I was opposed to school.
And now, again,
I'm opposed to work.

Above all it is health
And righteousness that I hate the most.
There's nothing so cruel to man
As health and honesty.

Of course I'm opposed to 'the Japanese spirit'
And duty and human feeling make me vomit.
I'm against any government anywhere
And show my bum to authors' and artists' circles.

When I'm asked for what I was born,
Without scruple, I'll reply, 'To oppose.'
When I'm in the east
I want to go to the west.

I fasten my coat at the left, my shoes right and left.
My *hakama*[108] I wear back to front and I ride a horse facing its
    buttocks.
What everyone else hates I like
And my greatest hate of all is people feeling the same.

This I believe: to oppose
Is the only fine thing in life.
To oppose is to live.
To oppose is to get a grip on the very self.

MIYAZAWA KENJI

November Third

Bending neither to the rain
Nor to the wind
Nor to snow nor to summer heat,
Firm in body, yet
Without greed, without anger,
Always smiling serenely.
Eating his four cups of rough rice a day
With bean paste and a few vegetables,
Never taking himself into account
But seeing and hearing everything,
Understanding
And never forgetting.
In the shade of a pine grove
He lives in a tiny thatched hut:
If there is a sick child in the east
He goes and tends him:
If there is a tired mother in the west
He goes and shoulders her rice sheaves:
If there is a man dying in the south
He goes and soothes his fears:
If there are quarrels and litigation in the north
He tells them, 'Stop your pettiness.'
In drought he sheds tears,
In cold summers he walks through tears.

Everyone calls him a fool.
Neither praised
Nor taken to heart.

That man
Is what I wish to be.

YAGI JŪKICHI

I first saw my face in a dream
On a night when my fever had been high for some time.
I had gone to sleep praying to Christ
And a face was revealed.
Not, of course, my face nowadays
Nor my face when I was young
Nor the face of the noblest of the angels
As I always picture it in my mind.
It was a face surpassing even this –
And I knew at once it was my own.

About the face was a gold-tinged blackness.
The next day when my eyes opened
The fever raged no less,
But in my heart was a strange calm.

MARUYAMA KAORU

Sorrow of parting

In the ear of an anchor, a gull croaks.
Suddenly, without a word, the anchor glides down.
Startled, the seagull takes off.
In a moment, the anchor turns pale in the water, sinking.
And what the seagull feels becomes a wild, sad scream
Lost in the wind.

Gun emplacement

Bits of shrapnel trying to huddle together:
A crack trying to burst its bonds:
A gun-barrel trying to rise
And sit on its carriage again.
Everything, dreaming of its passing original form
Was buried in sand with each blast.
Out of sight, the sea,
And the flickering gleam of migrating birds.

Wings

A seagull raced in through the window
Knocking over the lamp in the room,
And in the following darkness lost its senses.

A hope, once:
Its wings, stained by the tide,
Smell of some huge remorse.

MIYOSHI TATSUJI

Lake

A man has been drowned in this lake, they think:
That is why so many boats are out
Among the waterweed and rushes.
Where is it that the corpse is hidden?
Still no whistle signal that it's been found.
The wind moving, sighing.
Sculls and paddles cleaving the water.
The wind moving, sighing.
Scent of reed-roots, of crabs.
Isn't there someone who knows

That in this lake a man died at dawn?
Someone must know,
Even though the night is already coming on.

Thunder moth

After the thunder
The thunder moth comes to the village.
Covered with the pollen of the lilies
In the village headman's garden,
She flutters a little
By the police box at the crossroads.
Then, lofted on the wind,
She soars higher than the pasanias,
Higher than the alarm bell
Of the fire-tower.

On the grass

Goose running along the lane:
Shadow, too, running along the lane.

Goose running over the lawn:
Shadow, too, running over the lawn.

White goose and her shadow,
Running . . . running . . . running.

And . . . into the water she goes!

TAKAHASHI SHINKICHI

Beach rainbow

Heedless of the spray from the steaming waves,
The shell sleeps.
Buried in sand, rolled by the sand shifting as the tide shifts,

Not hearing the noise of the thundering waves,
The shell lies down lightly.

Some day, this beach too –
The earth's crust shifting – may turn into fields
Or perhaps into the floor of the sea.

The shell does not worry about the far future,
Does not covet the form of the clouds drifting in the sky,
Does not pine after its lost body parted by death.

Idly, not sobbing, not scurrying,
Resigned to the march of nature,
Without anguish, quietly drifting.

In a typhoon, bending its ear to the din:
Baked on the sand in the burning sun:
Picked up by a man in a daydream:
Turned into a button, even. Unconcerned.

Sea shell,
Beach rainbow,
Keep your eyes on your beautiful dream.

Birth

Did my hand ever touch your hair?
Did my fingers ever feel your soft skin?

Always between us a winter frost descended,
A summer haze drifted, didn't it?

Yet your belly, swollen with child,
Twitches and jumps with the quickening.

We slept between the same sheets, yet
I don't know who you are.
The child you will bear could be you
Or it might well be me.

And you, as well, don't know who I am.

Now you hold two lives: I can no more see you as an individual.
All your love is centred now on the child you will bear.
I, the father – my being is less important than the child's rearing.

This is illusion, perhaps:
Neither you nor I really exist:
Merely, through the sense of touch, at times we feel alive
Just as in a dream,
And our child will be born to this dream.

What's born doesn't live for ever
And what exists isn't reborn.
So, whether you exist or are something that's been born,
I do not know.

OKAMOTO JUN

Under the hazy, blossom-laden sky

Under the hazy, blossom-laden sky
The city sprawls, its gaping wounds exposed:
The streets due for a surgical operation,
Canals gathering pitch and filth,
Bridges with their concrete peeling away.

Under the hazy, blossom-laden sky
Cranes moving,
Drain-pipes lined up,
Truck after truck
Carrying dirt, rubbish, mud,
The burnt-out, festering hulks of war.

Dark caverns in the streets:
On the canal bed, submerged groans and sighs
Of those who will not surface:
Methane gushing up.

In the city with these clogged wounds
International streets will appear soon,
Rows of smart shops will grow,
Tempting goods will brighten the windows.

Under the hazy, blossom-laden sky
New building goes on.
Our ears tuned to the detonations under the hazy, blossom-laden
    sky,
We pray
That the fire-rain never again fall on the world.

Battlefield of dreams

When you were two or three
I stood in the garden holding you.
As I held you
I chased my dreams to the other end of the far sky.
With a start
You slipped from my arms and fell.
You cried terribly
And my dream world vanished away.
You grew up none the worse for wear
And went through primary school.
I, careless and inconsistent,
Decided not to hold you after that,
Left you all to your mother
And stopped worrying about the house,
Giving myself to my dreams.

You, the only child,
Loved your dolls, loved animals, loved plants.
Even more than a new doll
You cuddled your old one, legs and arms all tattered.
You talked with wild flowers whose names you didn't know.
Dogs, cats, birds, insects,
Anything wild you made friends with at once.
But your favourite was Impy, the stray dog.

Impy went to school with you,
Had his lessons in your arms.
In your fifth year at school,
The police took me off for some old thing.
You came with mother
Or, sometimes, alone to visit me.
'Here again,' you'd say,
Nonchalantly entering the room.

Grave old men laughed;
You, fond of paints,
Drew my face with all its growth
And the old men's heads, with no concern,
And set them all laughing.
One old man
Stuck his picture on the wall,
Making us laugh till we could laugh no more.
'I'll come again,' you'd say,
Waving your hand as you left.

Then at girls' high school,
Taller than your mother,
The most mischievous in the school, they said.
Apt to be
Stubborn as a mule;
Once you'd decided,
You never let go.
This obstinacy in you
I watched, silently.
Three, five, ten years hence
What will become of you
I don't know.
Whether happy or unhappy
I cannot say,
For happiness and unhappiness
Do not enter my world.

Your dream, fast asleep and clasping your tattered doll,
With its dirty finger-marks,
Eyes and nose crumpled,
And my dream as I dropped you and woke you.

Impact of dream on dream
Mingling
Violent
Burning
Reckless
Roaring din.

And on the battlefield
Of quiet dreams,
Amid the swirling cannon smoke,
A tiny gentleness,
A flower that does not wither.

MURANO SHIRŌ

Black song

From eyes, from ears,
Blackness pours;
Melted in the night,
Flesh gushing from my mouth.
What can it be,
This black song?

Here no dawn reaches:
A vacuum
In the earth's shade,
No tree, house, dog.
And here, a heart
That will not die,
That will not sleep,
Singing, singing.

Friends of the world,
Listen to its song,
Black song of peace.

The flesh

Plump servant of the spirit,
You are a vase dripping away,
Its tender lip filled with god's spittle.

You are a lewd shed
Where animals lie together.

Now, you are a chapel without a priest
And now, like a lonely home that has a nurse.

Or the bare frame of an instrument,
Its springs stretched.

And, across a space scored with scars,
Flowing far away,
A landscape.

Present winter

He
From the world out there
Walks by my side.

Sometimes, near noon,
Disappearing in the wheels on the road;
Then revealed over on the far hill,
Making a sound of iron hands,
A sound of iron feet.
Who in the world
Is the man in that harsh vision?

The frontiers of the two worlds
Cold, like glass.
The winter sun dimly refracted there:
White phantoms, too,
Appearing from several decades ago.

Sometimes in the world out there,
The sound of cannon
Beating on the surface of the clear glass.

That white shadow –
Would it be man: or new spirit?

His back turned,
He re-enters the world out there;
On his white back, clear,
Shadows of the branches of winter trees.

Beggar

His rags glint in the sun:
Yet his poverty is so clear,
Tangled in his tatters,
That it shines through everything
Like a kernel, like a core,
With everything else dissolved.

After a while he moves
From one thin shaft of sun
To a new one, taking his time.

One piece of existence moves,
Trailing its soul behind
Like an unhappy child.

NAKANO SHIGEHARU

The Imperial Hotel

1

Here, it's the West:
The dogs talk English.
Here, manners are the West's:
The dogs invite you to Russian opera.
Here, it's the West, the West's bazaar:
A junkshop of Japanese fly-blown clothes and curios.

Here, too, is a gaol:
The warder twiddles his keys.
Yes, here a dank and cheerless gaol:
Warder and prisoner speak to no man.
Prisoners are known by numbers:
A warder stands by the door.

Here, it's a cheap bar:
Fat men get tight.

Here, it's a whorehouse:
Whores parade in the nude.

Here, it's a nothing
Black and stinking.

2

Huge nothing
Huge whorehouse
Huge bar parlour
Huge dank gaol.
A seedy junkshop of Japan
Squats in the heart of Tokyo
And vomits a vile stink
Over all our heads.

Song

Don't sing of crimson flowers or wings of the dragonfly,
Of the wind's whispers or the scent in a woman's hair.
All that is delicate,
All that is vague,
All that is languid — away with it!
All that is elegant — out with it!
Sing, instead, of what is fair and square,
Of what helps the heart.
Stick out your chest and sing;
Sing fit to burst your lungs.
Under fire, sing the rebound song,
The song that plucks courage
From the depth of shame.
Swell your throat and sing
These songs
In strict rhythm.
Din them in
The hearts of all.

Farewell before dawn

We have our work.
To work, we must talk,
But if we talk
The police come and batter in our faces.

So we switched our upper room,
With an eye to a back alley and escape route.
Six young men asleep here
And, beneath, a couple and their baby.
I don't know the past of these six;
I only know they think as I do.
I don't know the names of the people below;
I only know they gladly rented their upper room.

Dawn any moment.
Moving on again,
Our bags all ready.
There'll be a secret meeting
And slowly our work will go forward.
Tomorrow, sleeping again in hired blankets.
Dawn any moment.
Good-bye, tiny room,
Nappies on the line,
Naked, grimy light,
Celluloid toys,
Hired blankets,
Bugs.
Good-bye!
That thoughts may flower –
Ours,
The couple's,
The baby's –
All, at once, and savagely.

Tokyo Imperial University students

Sallow faces
Spectacles
Haoris[109]
Rubashkas
Overcoats with buttons an inch wide
Some who look like beggars
Some who swagger along *Ginza*[110]
Some who get drunk and deliberately use foul provincialisms.
Profound learning
Character building
'*The Symbol of Anguish* – not bad, is it?'[111]
Yah.
Streaming through the main gate.
Some just kick a football.

KUSANO SHIMPEI

Mount Fuji, Opus 5

Flame of fire mountain
Reflecting red in the snow,
Gentle flame, reflecting on the snow's shoulder,
Flame, standing calmly in the sky,
Snuffed in the thick of the night.

Look – there, above it,
Straight above it, among the open spaces on the moon,
In great spirals, winds a blue-green cord.

Drawing near,
I would ask the dragon:

'Why should the ways of the world be sad?
Let the swirling clouds coil no longer,
Let the flames dazzle from your glittering scales . . .
Lula-lula-la . . .
Sharp eyes, sharp claws, close them, close them . . .
Lula-lula-la . . . See how it coils!'

Stone

Wax-tree, five-needled pine,
Grow from a fissure.

Sodden after the rain,
Moss flowers reflected in a granite skin.

At the deep, silent
Base of coming and going

Ants and mushrooms,
Temple of hill and river spirits.
Clouds drawn up to the blue skies.

Hemmed round by dripping grasses,
Bluntly the stone glimmers.

KONDŌ AZUMA

Mediterranean woman

The girl's back, reflected upside down in the mirror,
was shiny as a wax match. The chestnut hair at the
tip of her smooth back was like lighted phosphorus.

She dropped her powder-puff on the sheet. The creases
in the sheet were like a chart of the Mediterranean
in April.

The girl was transported, telling the streets of her
home with her body – the steep road to the harbour,
the wine, a concertina: a shower, even, falling on
her polished skin.

The powder-puff was thrown from the window. Thrown
from the window, it fell like a flower, with the
smell of the Mediterranean spring.

Fire

The distant range of the mountains, like a shark's lower jaw,
Bared its fangs to heaven.
Shapes of people turning into crows.
Blackness of night covering everything.
   No newspaper
   No watch
   But a vast expanse of bean-field.
I was flurried, as if I had strayed into the age of the gods.
But
Now and again the latest warplanes flew overhead in formation
And I heard the sound of Skoda machine-guns.

I asked
Do you have hope?
He did not reply.

What do you have?
He pointed to his garden:
There, stacked or scattered,
Was dried ox-dung.

What is that?
Fire!
Fire?
A cake of dung
Under a huge cauldron
Was burning, white, red.

He and I
For the first time laughed the laugh of god and man,
Laughed the laugh of god and man.

TAKENAKA IKU

Story

Quietly the cloud cast its shadow,
Passing over avenues of trees, over ponds, over fields.
Enduring both joy and sadness, the cloud silently drifted on . . .

Then, above the sound of a single flute, the cloud stopped,
Seeking the one who played: but there was no one.

And then the cloud began again its long journey
Through the hemisphere of night, not knowing its direction.

Thinking stone

There is a three-cornered stone, white even in the dark,
In the centre of the pitch-black square
Just like Rodin's 'Thinker'
The granite like a man with his chin on his fist.

You are thinking
Of the daytime and the man who sat down on you
Of the daytime and the child who tripped against you
Of the daytime and the blind man who knocked his stick on you.

The man who sat down on you despaired of living
The child who tripped against you groaned with hunger
The blind man's stick was shattered in pieces.

I strike a match reluctant to catch alight
And put it near you.
Your quartz, your felspar, your mica
Glitter and blink and seem to want to speak.

Stars

Over Japan there are stars.
Stars that stink like petrol
Stars that speak with foreign accents
Stars that rattle like old Fords
Stars the colour of Coca-Cola
Stars that hum like a fridge
Stars as coarse as tinned food
Stars cleaned with cotton wool and tweezers
And sterilized with formalin
Stars charged with radioactivity.
Among them, stars too swift for the eye
And stars circling on an eccentric orbit.
Deep down
They plunge to the base of the universe.

Over Japan there are stars.

On wintry nights –
Every night –
They stretch like a heavy chain.

Tourist Japan

Fujiyama – we sell.
Miyajima – we sell.
Nikkō – we sell.
Japan – we sell anywhere.
Naruto, Aso –
We sell it all.[112]
Prease, prease, come and view!
Me rub hands,
Put on smile.
Money, money – that's the thing!
We Japanese   all buy cars
We Japanese   all like lighters
We Japanese   all good gardeners
We Japanese   all sing pops.
All of us bow,
All, all, are meek and mild. Yes!

HARA TAMIKI

In the fire, a telegraph pole
At the heart of the fire.
A telegraph pole like a stamen,
Like a candle,
Blazing up, like a molten
Red stamen.
In the heart of the fire on the other bank
From this morning, one by one,
Fear has screamed
Through men's eyes. At the heart of the fire
A telegraph pole, like a stamen.

Glittering fragments

Glittering fragments
Ashen embers
Like a rippling panorama,
Burning red then dulled.
Strange rhythm of human corpses.
All existence, all that could exist
Laid bare in a flash. The rest of the world
The swelling of a horse's corpse
At the side of an upturned train,
The smell of smouldering electric wires.

NAKAHARA CHŪYA

Leaves of the fig-tree

Summer morning. Fig-leaves,
Leaves withered, drowsy-coloured,
Rattling in the wind,
Trembling on weak branches.

Shall I go to sleep?
Electric cables reach to the sky,
And from the cables, songs of far cicadas.
Leaves withered,
Rattling in the wind;
Leaves trembling, branches tilting.

Shall I go to sleep?
Sky dark and still,
Sun tangled in the clouds,
Electric cables striking the sky.

Cicadas in the distance.
Everyone I love gone.

Cold night

On a winter night
My heart is sad
Sad for no reason
My heart is rusty, purple.

Beyond the heavy door
Past days are vague
On top of the hill
Cotton seeds burst open.

Here firewood smoulders
Smoke climbs from it
As if it even knows itself.

Without being invited
Or even wishing
My heart smoulders.

The Marunouchi Building [113]

Ah! lunch and
There goes the siren,
There goes the siren.
Out they stream,
Out they stream.

Salarymen out for lunch,
Aimlessly swinging arms.
And still out they stream,
Out they stream.

Vast building,
Coal-black tiny
Tiny exit.

Thin cloud filming the sky,
Thin cloud and
Dust blowing up.

Comical salarymen
Looking up,
Looking down.

Why should I be
The great man that
I know I am?

Ah! lunch and
There goes the siren,
There goes the siren.

Out they stream,
Out they stream.

Vast building,
Coal-black tiny
Tiny exit.

The siren mounts on the wind,
Echoes, re-echoes, and blows away.

TACHIHARA MICHIZŌ

Afterthoughts

My dreams always returned
To a lonely village at the foot of a mountain;
Wind sighing over the knot-grass,
Skylark singing and singing,
To a forest path in quiet noon.

In the blue sky, sun shining clear,
Volcano asleep,
And I
Talking of what I have seen – islands, breakers, headlands, sun,
    and moonlight;
Even though I knew none listened,
Talking, talking . . .

Here the dream stops short.
I try to forget everything –
And when I forget even that I have forgotten,
The dream will freeze in midwinter's memories
And, opening the door,
Recede along the path lit by the Milky Way.

Night song of a traveller

Cold rain swirls savagely,
The lantern in my hand hardly
Pierces the gloom at my feet,
Walking through endless night.

Why should I be walking?
I have put them aside – engulfing
Bed, warm talk, light. But
Why should I be walking?

When dawn comes, before I sleep,
Where should I get to? And, once there,
What should I do?

Wet through to the skin –
But, wet, I recall
Only good memories.

Shall I go home?
Or shall I go down
That street of red lights?
No. Into the darkness.

KINOSHITA YŪJI

Late summer

The pumpkin tendrils creep
Along the station platform.
A ladybird peeps
From a chink in the half-closed flowers.

A stopping train comes in.
No one gets on, or off.

On the millet stalk
Growing by the railing
The young ticket-man
Rests his clippers.

KURODA SABURŌ

I've changed completely

I've changed completely
Yes I'm wearing the same tie as yesterday
I'm as poor as yesterday
As useless as yesterday
Even so I've changed completely.
Yes I'm wearing the same clothes as yesterday
I'm as blind drunk as yesterday
As clumsy as yesterday
Even so I've changed completely.

Ah
Faced with all the half smiles and grins
Curled sneers and guffaws
I shut my eyes tight and stay still
And
Fluttering through me towards tomorrow
Goes a beautiful white butterfly.

YOSHIOKA MINORU

Still life

Night closes in
Bones
Placed for a moment
Among the fish
Steal from the star-lit sea
And decompose secretly
On the dish.

The light
Shifts to another dish
In whose hollow
Lurks only living famine
Summoning first the shadow
And then the seed.

Past

Apron dangling from his thin neck
He has no purpose and no past
A sharp knife in one hand he starts to walk
Beyond the corner of his wide-open eyes a file of ants scurries
      across the floor
Disturbing the dust illuminated in the knife blade
A plate of food

A chamber pot
Its substance screaming
Suddenly blood flowing through the window to the sun
Now what has waited patiently for him
Gives him the past
Which he lacked
Stingray lying unmoving on the table
Speckled broad-backed slippery
Tail seeming to hang down to the cellar
Beyond only winter rain roofs
He nimbly rolls up his apron sleeves
Plunges the knife in the stingray's belly
No resistance
No response
To butchery
Hand unstained – horrifying
However he exerts strength and splits the membrane
Dark depths with nothing to spew out
Stars now shining now dim
Work done he takes his hat from the wall
Hidden till now by the hat
From the nail shielded from terror
Blood heavy and round as full time slowly gushes.

Saffron gathering

On a palace wall in Crete
They say there is a sumptuous mural
Called 'Saffron Gathering'
A boy on all fours
Gathers saffron
Blue-green waves repeat whirlpool patterns among rocks day by
    day
But if the sun were to strike the boy's forehead
When we see him only from behind
Star-patterned salt would float to the surface
When on an evening headland the boy's split buttocks

Are thrust out
We recognize the trickle of the fragrant juice of saffron stalk
Waves come   white choppy waves
Next the beheaded
Neck of a beautiful monkey will be decked out
Above the quartz-like pitch-dark face
Of the boy, his eyes shut
Like an Arcimboldi portrait
Made up of fruits of spring and fish
Everything decomposes
From the surface
The monkey's torso lapped by
Creeds and curses beneath the Aegean Sea
In the night which a virgin's body cannot resist
Rustling dead blue-green hair
Is it the thighs of his wet-nurse?
Is it the hidden penis of the monkey?
This is supported on the boy's moist shoulders
Reflected in the mirror
Like a hieroglyph
Sunset glow tints the columns
Waves die down
Circling, circling inside a brown shell
'Song' is born
Pale violet of saffron flowers
Were someone to entice him
Rushing down the ledge the boy
Will borrow the form of drowning from several types of syncope
For the moment we shall not tell
Should not tell
That story about the swimming monkey
Until the day when waves wash over the canopy of heaven.

ISHIGAKI RIN

Living

I can't live without eating
Rice
Vegetables
Meat
Air
Light
Water
Parents
Brothers and sisters
Teachers
Money too and heart
I couldn't have come through alive without eating
Holding my bloated belly
Wiping my mouth
Carrot peelings
Chicken bones
Father's guts
Scattered around in the kitchen
For the first time in forty sunsets
Beast's tears brimming in my eyes.

TAMURA RYŪICHI

October poem

Crisis is part of me.
Beneath my smooth skin
Is a typhoon of savage passion. On October's
Desolate shore a fresh corpse is thrown up.

October is my empire.
My gentle hands control what is lost
My small eyes keep watch on what is melting
My soft ears listen to the silence of the dying.

Terror is part of me.
In my rich bloodstream
Courses all-killing time. In October's
Chilling sky a fresh famine shudders.

October is my empire.
My dead troops occupy every rain-sodden city
My dead patrol-plane circles the sky over
                         aimless minds
My dead people sign their names for the dying.

Three voices

The voice came from the distance
The voice came from the far distance
Lower than all whispers
Louder than all shrieks
Deeper than the depths of history
Far deeper than the 10,830 metres of the Emden Sea
Sea within words
Piercing lost seas discovered only by poets
Splitting the world's coldest air
Sinking on the seabed the world's most delicate squadron
Controller of our kings and the cities of our senses
Re-creator of our dead sailors and our fatigue
The voice came from the distance
The voice came from the far distance.

Oh because
We cannot commit crimes
We are the statistics of terror, statistics of terror
We are the proclamation of lust, proclamation of lust
We cannot commit crimes

Oh because
We are not individuals
We are the herd, the crowd
We are the crowd itself.

The voice came through a tear
The voice came through a single tear
Poorer than all who are poor
Dearer than all who are dear
Fiercer than the heart's white heat
Far fiercer than the sorrow of him who died alone two thousand
    years ago
Love within words
Piercing lost love discovered only by poets
Glittering in the world's most seething cascade
Plunging down the world's most parched throat
Violator of our energies and our skin
Wrecker of our faiths and our kisses
The voice came through a tear
The voice came through a single tear.

Oh because
We cannot destroy with love
We are the invention of passion, invention of passion
We are the news of crisis, news of crisis
We cannot destroy with love
Oh because
We are not solitary
We are the herd, the crowd
We are the crowd itself.

The voice came through time
The voice came through a single time
With a future more gloomy than all pasts
With a past more glittering than all futures
Sharper than the charity of a deity
Far sharper than the light of the Charioteer passing through the
    February meridian at eight pm Tokyo Central Standard Time

Time within words
Piercing lost time discovered only by poets
Kissing the world's most pallid cheeks
Dropping the evening sun on the world's most desolate horizons
Plunderer of our corpses and our deserted stations
Perjurer of our science and our blood
The voice came through time
The voice came through a single time.

Oh because
We cannot die
We are the advertisement of immortality, advertisement of
    immortality
We are the policy of dissipation, policy of dissipation
We cannot die
Oh because
We are not alone
We are the herd, the crowd
We are the crowd itself.

I hear the voice
And at last I will bear my mother
They hear the voice
And our corpses shall attack vultures
She hears the voice
And my mother shall bear death.

Four thousand days and nights

For a single poem to be born
We have to kill
We have to kill many
Shoot, murder, poison many whom we love.

Look!
From the sky of four thousand days and nights
All because we need the quivering tongue of one tiny bird
We have shot

The silence of four thousand nights, the counter-light of four
  thousand days.

Listen!
From all the rain-soaked cities and blast furnaces
From the midsummer wharves and coal mines
All because we want the tears of just one starving child
We have murdered
The love of four thousand days, the pity of four thousand nights.

Remember!
All because we need the terror of a single stray dog
Which sees what we cannot see
Which hears what we cannot hear
We have poisoned
The imagination of four thousand nights, the cold memory of four
  thousand days.

For a single poem to be born
We have to kill those we love
This is our one way to bring back the dead
And this is the way we must do it.

Far-off land

My suffering
Is simple
  Like keeping an animal from a far-off land
  There's no real need for a groom.

My poetry
Is simple
  Like reading a letter from a far-off land
  There's no real need for tears.

My joys and sorrows
Are still more simple
  Like killing a man from a far-off land
  There's no real need for words.

YOSHINO HIROSHI

For my first child

The day right after you were born

Like vultures
Those men showed up
Opening and closing
Their black leather briefcases.

They were life insurance salesmen

'Your ears are very sharp'
I showed my surprise
They laughed and replied
'The scent reached us.'

With your face not even formed
On your tender body
Where
Would I have awarded
A tiny death?

Already
Its fragrant scent
Is drifting here – did they not say?

Sunset glow

As always
The train was full
And
As always
A young man and a girl sat down
An old man was left standing
The girl looked away
And offered the old man her seat
Brusquely he sat down

With not a word of thanks the old man got off at the next station
The girl sat down
Another old man was shoved
In front of the girl
The girl looked away
But
Again she stood up
And offered her seat
To the old man
The old man thanked her as he got off at the next station
The girl sat down
It never rains but it pours . . . as they say
Another man was shoved
In front of the girl
Poor old thing
The girl looked away
And this time did not offer her seat
At the next stop
And the next one
Biting her lower lip
Stiffening her body
I got off the train
Turning hard-hearted and looking away
How far could she have gone?
Those who possess kind hearts
Always and everywhere
Sacrifice themselves involuntarily
Why, you ask?
Because those who possess kind hearts
Feel
Others' pain as their own
Feeling blame in her kind heart
How far could the girl have gone?
Biting her bottom lip
In a bitter mood
And missing the beautiful sunset glow.

IBARAGI NORIKO

The fruit

On a high branch
A big green fruit
A local lad slid up
Stretched his hand and fell back
What looked like fruit
Was a moss-covered skull.

Mindanao[114]
Twenty-six years on
On a baby jungle tree branch
Caught by chance
The skull of a Japanese soldier killed in battle
Eye socket nostril
In the sturdy young tree
Grown vigorously.

In his lifetime
This face
Irreplaceable cherished
Surely some woman must have cared for it.

The fontanelles of the tiny temples
Who was the mother who had doted on them
Twining her fingers in his hair?
Who was the woman who had drawn him tenderly to her?
If it had been me . . .

I broke off a year has passed
I took the draft out again
Unable to find a final line
More years have gone by.

If it had been me
In the end unable to produce a line to follow.

When I looked my prettiest

When I looked my prettiest
Streets were bare crumbling
From unexpected places
You could see blue skies.

When I looked my prettiest
Many around me died
In factories at sea on islands with no name
I missed the chance to dress up.

When I looked my prettiest
No one was tender and gave me presents
Men knew only how to give a salute
All went off leaving only pure looks.

When I looked my prettiest
I was empty-headed
I was hard-hearted
Only hands and feet shone chestnut brown.

When I looked my prettiest
My country was defeated in war
That could never be
I rolled up my blouse sleeves and strutted our mean streets.

When I looked my prettiest
Jazz spilled from the radio
I felt giddy as when I broke no-smoking rules
I craved the sweet music of an alien land.

When I looked my prettiest
I was very unhappy
I was all topsy-turvy
I was *horribly* lonely

So I've decided if I can to live a long life
When I'm old painting *awfully* beautiful pictures[115]
Like France's old M. Rouault
Yes?

IIJIMA KŌICHI

Mother tongue

During my half year abroad
I never once thought
About writing poems
I moved about
Unaware of myself
Asked why I didn't write poems
I could never answer.

I came back to Japan
And after a while
I couldn't but write poems
Now at last
I understand that half year
I could move about not writing poems
It's that I am home again
Inside my mother tongue.

Inside the words mother tongue
Are 'mother' and 'country' and 'tongue'
During the half year that I persuaded myself that I was cut off
From mother and country and tongue
I walked through the real world
Immune from injury
The need was hardly there
For me to write poems.

In April Paul Celan
Drowned himself in the Seine
I feel I understand
The act of this poet who was Jewish
Poems are sad
They say that poetry sets right one's mother tongue
It's not so for me
Every day I suffer injury by my mother tongue
Every night I must set out
For another mother tongue
That makes me write poems, gives me life.

Stranger's sky

The birds have returned
Pecking at cracks in the dark earth
Soaring and swooping
On strange roofs
As if bewildered.

The sky holds its head as if it had swallowed a stone
Lost in its thoughts
There was no outflow
So the blood circles
The sky like a stranger.

KAWASAKI HIROSHI

Animal nightmares

Dogs and
Horses
Seem to have dreams.

Animal
Nightmares
Seem to have no humans.

ŌOKA MAKOTO

Song of the flame

When he touches me
He shrieks with terror
Yet I do not know
If I am hot or cold
I do not stay in the same position even for an instant
For what I was a moment ago no longer exists
I always go on my way burning.

I set myself against the dark
Yet the home I go back to
Is always in the dark.

Men are frightened of me
Because without knowing why
I like trees paper human flesh come close to them
Snuggle them fondle them drink them dry
Since I myself
Die out over their ashes
Piercing indifferently
The shrieks of those who have touched me
Teach me how
The fondness that I have for men
Is the focus of their fear.

For spring

You dig for spring drowsing in the sands
And deck your hair with it you laugh
Laughter-foam like ripples scattered to the sky
Sea serenely warming grass-green sun.

Your hand on mine
The stone you throw in my sky
Petal-shadows flowing down today's sky-bed.

New shoots sprout in our arms
In the centre of our view
Gold sun revolving sending up spray
We are lake we are trees
We are sunlight dappling through trees on the lawn
Dappled sunlight dancing on the terrace of your hair.

In the fresh wind a door opens
An enormous hand summons us and the green shadows
Roads are fresh on the earth's tender skin
Your arms glisten in the fountain
Under our eyelashes bathed in sunlight
Sea and fruit
Ripen serenely.

Words words

I

I keep on vacant land
A horse which none can see
Now and again grasping the reins
I go to meet a twelfth-century Zen priest
He lived for eight hundred years
There is no trace of his body
His body has turned into words
Soon even the words will be gone
Until then a temporary home
Borrowing the eaves of words
'Flowers open and the world arises'
When he says this
He is the flowers opening he is the world arising
As words within words along with words
Opening and closing
Floating and sinking
Born killed
Continuing as words
Continuing to live inside words

Unable to die
While words exist on earth
He turns into rocks wheels love
He transforms into blood sky calendar
And so he must continue to be tortured
By the painful recognition that he is the world's equal
What is it that is painful
There is no pain like
That of words become flesh
That mankind does not feel it as pain
Is because they do not truly feel the flesh
Says the withered priest.

2

Everyone jabbered with difficult words
So realizing that unless I became a parrot
I would be out of tune
I felt ill and sank into sleep
But then a horde of lips came to my bedside
And complained 'What nasty words you use
Thanks to you our ears are on fire'
How crazy I thought and got to my feet
'Right then, shall we compare your words
And mine and let us build all the Romes after that'
I said and turned to my desk searching it for words
Not a single word
Not in the room
On the street   on the rim of the picture frame   inside the cables
Nor in my mouth in my fingers
So all were stunned and turned into stone pillars.

Turned to stone I stood for a while
Seasons revolved winds revolved
Seeds revolved in my pores
Rain gathered in the hollows
Sound invisibly thin swiftly piled up
The sun shone   the landscape changed   the streets changed

I stood silent for an age
The sounds around me began to awaken began to burgeon
The sound of the wind swelled into an intolerable storm
Growing seeds reverberating with a crash
The sound of rain gathering like a moaning bullet
The sound of sand piling up like a hammer striking a coffin
Even the sun's rays made a sound as they fell.

I stood silent
In an ocean of silence
Plankton of sounds
Began to make shrill heartbeats reverberate
'Listen   these are words   nature's words'
I screamed like a madman   I looked about me
And not a soul
In the room constellations floating
In the forest of the wind sounds burning
In this moment of ecstasy
I hung
Tilting towards a murky river
Straining my eyes
Buffeted by waves far below
Vast writings
Vast varieties of paper
Slowly sinking
Never to appear again.

SHIRAISHI KAZUKO

Street

Dark street   seedy town
Raining   a bit too cold
We wore raincoats   we had a black umbrella
However much we signalled, the taxis didn't stop
So we set off walking

Our bodies close, clinging
What kind of future did we face
As we walked, drenched to the skin?

Warm hotel
Bodies
Heated
But the words
And acts of our loving –
I cannot recall
A single one.

Pond

'Go home,' I said
'Tonight I don't want you, so
Go home,' I said
Sniffling and sobbing
You went off
I have no place to go back to.

Your path as you went weeping from my heart
I traced again and again
Your tear stains
Spread across my body
To become a pond
And that pond engulfed my heart
That night I went to sleep.

Memories of Joe

Billie's drinking Scotch
Billie's drinking Scotch.

Joe's gone off
Joe's gone away
Joe's gone far away
Joe's gone to jail

Why? Don't know
Maybe he got happy, picked a quarrel
Perhaps he got happy –
But it wasn't such a big deal –
Or so he wrote in his letter
'I had a good time
But not all that good.'

'His head's like a peanut, I don't fancy him'
Said June, and she went off, left Joe
Joe took it badly, that's for sure
Still, it wasn't Joe's fault
His head was that shape; that apart
He was pretty handsome
Full of fun and
A basketball champion and
Sang well, danced well
But there was one thing
I couldn't forget about him
He had a huge appetite
Mrs Green used to say
'Can't keep a thing in the fridge when he's around'
Mrs Green had only to turn her back
And Joe would get his hands on her kebabs
Even so he's not a bad chap
He plays Indians with her kids and lets them kill him
He'll always chat up a pretty girl, give her a kiss
Good at judo
Muscly legs
The real thing much better than it looks.

Billie's drinking Scotch
For a while now, drinking Scotch.

Yesterday there was a letter from his brother Bobby
Bobby is Billie's twin brother
You might think there's only one chap in the world
As strange as Billie, but there's another

It's a queer feeling: but nowadays
They're quite different
'Different lifestyles
Bobby had a baby; I haven't
Because I'm not married
Because I've not made one
Maybe I can't make one, maybe there's no seed; no, it's not that,
    it's her, she's bad, I'll stop doing it with her, Scotch is better
I'll drink Scotch, then bit by bit
I'll understand what it is that's inside Billie
It's Scotch, Billie knows it's Scotch.'

Brother Bobby said
'Our kid sister had twins not long ago'
She was always saying she wanted twins and she had twins
I wonder how you get twins
Don't know what you have to do
You won't know till you've tried a bit more Scotch.

'Muriel, Muriel, Muriel'
Muriel – I've heard that name somewhere
Muriel – it's not her
Before I was born she's been living inside me and as long as I live
    it's a name that will stay with me
Muriel
And quick as a flash she's by my side
'Billie, whatever's happened?'
Oh hell
It's not you
It's a different other Muriel, another Muriel.

I cling to my dream Muriel, hug her closer
Joe's gone
Maybe the Joe I know won't come back, the 21-year-old Joe I
    know
Like the elusive dream Muriel
Will turn into a different Joe.

Billie's drinking Scotch
Billie's drinking Scotch.

June 18th 1962 will never come back.

Billie?
Billie's drinking Scotch
Couldn't care less, cool, on the outside at least
Billie's drinking Scotch
Drinking Scotch.

TANIKAWA SHUNTARŌ

When the wind is strong

When the wind is strong,
The earth seems like someone's kite.
But as it is still high noon,
Men notice that night is already there.

The wind uses no words,
But only frets as it swirls about.
I think of the winds on other stars,
Whether they could be friends together.

On the earth, there is night, there is day.
Between them, what are the stars doing?
Silent, spreading. How do they endure?

In the daylight, the blue sky tells lies.
While the night mutters the truth, we are asleep.
And in the morning, we all say we dreamed.

The isolation of two billion light years

Mankind, on its little ball
Sleeps, wakes and works
Wishing at times for friendship with Mars.

Martians, on *their* little ball –
What they do I do not know
(Maybe they *sloop*, *wike* and *wook*)
But at times they wish for friendship with Earth
That's certain.

Universal gravitation
Is the force of isolation pulling together.

The universe is deformed
So we all unite our wants.

The universe goes on expanding
So we all feel uneasy.

At the isolation of two billion light years
Unconsciously, I sneezed.

Growing up

Three, and
There is no past for me.

Five, and
My past goes back to yesterday.

Seven, and
My past goes back to my topknot.

Eleven, and
My past goes back to dinosaurs.

Fourteen, and
My past is as the text books say.

Sixteen, and
I look timidly at the infinity of my past.

Eighteen, and
I know no more of time.

Family

Elder sister,
Who is it coming, in the loft?

It is we who are coming.

Elder sister
What is it ripening, on the stairs?

It is we who are ripening, young brother:
You and I, father and mother,
Outside, in the drought,
We are working.

Who is it eating
The bread on the table?

It is we who are eating,
Tearing at it with our nails.

Then, who is it drinking
Your blood, elder sister?

It's a man you do not know,
A tall man, with a nice voice.

Elder sister, elder sister,
In the barn there, what did you do?

He and I performed an incantation,
Lest all of us might die.

And so?

And so
My breasts will grow full
For the sake of one more of us.

Who is that?

It is you, it is I,
It is father and mother.

Who will come, then, at night
When we say our prayers?

   No one.

Above the weathercock?

   No one.

Beyond the dust in the road?

   No one.

In the evening, by the well-side?

   We are all here.

Sadness

Near where you hear the blue sky-waves
I think I mislaid
Something quite valuable.

In a station clearly in the past
Standing in front of the lost-property attendant
I felt even more sad.

Nero
For a loved little dog

Nero
Summer will soon be here again
Your tongue
Your eyes
The way you looked as you napped at noon
Now live vividly again for me.

You knew only two summers
I've known eighteen summers already
And now I remember all manner of summers
      some mine   some not mine.

The summer of Maison Lafitte
The summer of Yodo
The summer of Williamsburg Bridge
The summer of Oran
Then I wonder
However many summers might mankind have known by now.

Nero
Summer will soon be here again
But it will be a summer without you
A different summer
A very different summer.

A new summer is on the way
And I will learn all manner of things
Beautiful things   ugly things
Things to cheer me things to sadden me
So I ask
Whatever is it?
Whyever is it?
Whatever should we do?

Nero
You died
You ran off on your own no one knows where
Your bark
Your touch
Your moods even
Now live vividly again for me.

But Nero
Summer will soon be here again
A new infinitely vast summer will be here
And
I shall be walking
To greet the new summer   to greet autumn   to greet winter
To greet spring   looking forward to a new summer again

To learn all that is new
And
To answer all my questions myself.

Sonnet 62

The world loves me
Sometimes brutally
Sometimes gently
So I can live for ever on my own.

Even when she first gave herself to me
I only heard the sounds of the world
For me only simple sadness and pleasure are clear
Because I am always of the world.

I fling myself
At sky, at trees, at her
That I might become the richness itself of the world.

. . . I call to her
The world turns to look
And I am gone.

NAKAE TOSHIO

Night and fish

Fish at night
Sense themselves drifting away
Beyond the earth
As the water level falls,
Shaking their tails and fins wildly
As the night is too quiet:
Conscious of the noise of splashing water,
Thinking they will be heard by someone,
They peer into the night.

Then
They come across a water boatman
Spinning round and round,
As if it had wandered off many years ago,
Lost itself and forgot its plans.

TAKAHASHI MUTSUO

Dead boy

Never knowing love
From the fearful peak of childhood
Suddenly become a boy tumbled to a well's blackness
Dank water enfolds and strangles me
Freezing drilling boring
To my heart fish-cold and clammy
But inside quickening, growing like a flower
Stirring on the surface of the underground water
From the green horn between my thighs
Soon a helpless bud will sprout and climb
Parting heavy soil with delicate fingers
And a white face lonely as a tree
Will feel the hurt of dawn
I long for that day
When all that is dark in me becomes light.

Christ of the thieves
In memory of M

Christ of the thieves
Father of fatherless children
Lover of runaway girls.

Every Christmas time
In the church porch and in the sanctuary
Your stable birth is celebrated
Master.

Here a pitiable human being
Man unable to be man
Woman failed in being woman
Rent boy hemmed in by fingers of scorn.

Even on this blessed eve
No happy circle for me
Father, mother and brothers too
The whole world says it does not know me.

From the first floor to the third floor of the cheap apartment block
There are lights in every room: around the feast their shadows
    whisper.
Every doorway bursts with blessings
But at me they make faces.

And so I came here
It is seven o'clock now
Still a little early for mass
So I thought you might have your hands free.

You
Master of heaven and earth
You also hemmed in by scandalous rumours
Were alone on this earth.

No, no, never would I
Count myself your equal
My sorrows are a little like yours
And that gives consolation.

You pardoned the thieves
You rescued the woman of the streets
In the same way
Admit me to the company of your followers.

At the church porch, from beginning to end
I sang the liturgy in praise
I did not understand the meaning well
But I confess my grateful tears overflowed.

Most of all the prayer on the road to the cross
Was more than I deserved
How many times was I mocked, reviled?
How many times did I fall on the way?

Become the father of the homos
You of the boundless mercy
At street corners on doss-house steps
They tremble with friendship.

Father son and holy spirit in one body I praised your name
I praised also your very holy mother
Saint Peter, Saint Paul, Saint Augustine, Thomas Aquinas
Most of all I praised the handsome Saint Sebastian.

Vouchsafe your heaven
And small, small bliss
Grant me one manly lover.

YOSHIMASU GŌZŌ

Burning

Golden sword facing the sun
Ah
Pear blossom crossing star-face.

In a part of Asia
Where wind blows
Souls turn into wheels racing above clouds.

My will
Is something blind
Turning into sun into apple
Not similar to
Nipple sun apple paper pen ink dream
Turning into them.

If it could turn into a terrible rhythm.

Tonight you
In your sports car
Can you from the front tattoo the face
Of a shooting star you?

ISAKA YŌKO

Morning assembly

Dampened by rain
Smell of ironing
Even loose threads of steamy jumper-skirts
Twisted into box-pleats
Line up soberly.

Morning school grounds
Row upon row
Form a navy-blue stream
Pallid hands and feet lined up
Anaemic lips tight closed.

Yasuda not come yet
Nakahashi neither.

Gymnastics begin
In time with the instructor's commands
Squashing genitals as they stand on tiptoe
Socks wrinkling round ankles
On the chest of the duty-student the daily timetable

In the clouded sunshine
They climb slowly
Up the slope.

Stream disturbed
Skins a little flushed
Suppressed by navy-blue
Walking the dark corridor
Something soft greets them at the window
Cheeks stirring
Emotions rippling
They have come from far away.

Persimmons

The jaws of my trickery were out of joint
The evening is desolate
Because I am no more
The evening is desolate
I complained to a friend my age
I hate her now
I hate her but
I strain and jump up
And all the while
Peep over the neighbour's fence
Here on my side the evening begins with persimmons
Over there the tree has dropped its fruit
The stubborn fruit over there
Floats across the evening.

Fingers

When I was small
Dad stuck out his forefinger.
I grasped it with five hot fingers and walked
And let the panorama of the days go past.
Perhaps his forefinger
Possesses a rather faster pace.

Men slowly coil around me.
In the hollow in my palm heat gathers
And has a damp feeling.
I bend my five fingers
So that they lie side by side, with no gap.
By the condition of heat and damp
I measure them.
Year by year
My finger tips have got drier.

ASABUKI RYŌJI

96
I classify

I classify tales, names, seasons, food, books, trees, geography,
places, sounds, smells, time, plants, animals, minerals, people,
insects, bodies, astronomy, cosmos, weather, numbers, Chinese
characters, vocabulary, grammar, stimuli, shapes, conduct, actions,
sex, person, devils, communication, greetings, calendars, pleasure,
pain, rhythm, phonemes, medicines, fibres, furniture, ornaments,
light, scenery, discourse, likes, dislikes

I classify

tales: those with endings, those without

names: those that can be remembered, those that cannot,
                whispers in the ear, names that always tremble pleas-
                antly on the lips and those that do not

seasons: spring which gently eliminates people, summer with
                its brilliant pain, autumn burning the tea plants so that
                roadside trees are dyed yellow, autumn for ever damp,
                winter with closed doors

food: raw, rotten, cooked, solids and liquids, sweet and sour,
                nutritious and not nutritious

books:	by number only
trees:	giant trees, those that hug the ground, those that grow into layered shapes, those that do not drink water
geography:	mountain ranges at night, the sea rioting, rivers branching, blood-sucking soil, blood-spitting soil, isolated tropical islands, places where the sea is visible and not visible
places:	here and not here, thin closed rooms and thick closed rooms
sounds:	grainy and not grainy, those that attract and those that repel
smells:	the smell of morning fruit and water at night
time:	pale light, twilight, time continuing to exist now, time that is lost, time that one can touch and endless icy time
plants:	those that propagate, those that do not, stalks and roots
animals:	those that run away and those that curl into a ball
minerals:	those that sparkle and those that do not, those that burn and those that do not
people:	people who are people and people who are not people
insects:	those that fly and those that do not, or those that spew out gossamer for webs and those that do not, or those that build nests or those that do not, or those which have a transparent body and those that carry poison
bodies:	those that protrude and those that are sunken, those that have a surplus and those that have a deficiency, those one can touch and those one cannot touch, those that are fresh and those that are dry
astronomy:	moons and suns (this is very simple)

cosmos: macrocosmos and microcosmos (this also is very simple)

weather: rain on a holiday, rain falling on a window pane, rain wetting a woman's hair, a passing shower, snow falling on a botanical garden, on a garden, on a skyscraper, wind inviting sleep, wind before one wakens, autumn sunlight

numbers: those that can be counted, those that cannot be counted

Chinese characters: those that can be deciphered and those that cannot be deciphered, lines and dots

vocabulary: men's words and women's words, those that should be included in glossaries and those that should not

I classify

grammar: prescriptive and generative, that which can be stereotyped and that which cannot be stereotyped

stimuli: pleasant and disagreeable, or the retina and the tympanum, or undulating and trembling, chronic creepiness

shapes: regular and irregular

conduct: the indulgence of those who are gentle and the pleasantness of those who are swift, singular and plural

actions: you languidly stretching out, you languidly eating, you dressing bustlingly, you clumsily taking off your clothes

sex: what is tolerated and what is not, via the rectum and not via the rectum

person: you and I, just the two

devils: devils which understand human speech and devils which do not understand human speech

communication: light and dark, what arrives and does not

greetings: those who send and those who are sent to

calendars: lunar and solar, revolving calendars, rapid tear-off calendars

pleasure: closed pleasure and open pleasure

pain: vegetable pain and mineral pain

rhythm: three-four rhythm and other rhythms

phonemes: 'a' and 'i' or pleasure and pain

medicines: you leaning, you bending down, midsummer sunlight suddenly turning pallid, those that are absorbed, those that are injected, antipyretics and purgatives, those that alleviate pain and those that induce pain

fibres: those that one ties, those that one uses as whips, those that jot down and those that make love

I classify

furniture: night furniture, constellation and sex furniture

ornaments: those that cover or reveal, the hardness of the ear-rings in contact with your ear-lobes and the softness of the sweater in contact with your nipples, the silk of your underwear that is verified by my fingertips

light: summer and autumn light, light glancing off the sea and the pavement, and light which the skin absorbs first thing in the morning

scenery: rich and rarefied, full and vacant, paper and writing

discourse: that which is here and that which is not here, or statements that are easily repudiated or the superfluous words of tiny birds or 'I love you . . .' or

I classify

likes and dislikes, me and you, or that which is me and that which is you, or

ITŌ HIROMI

Under the earth

Through my marriage I was connected, so in August
I visited the grave for Bon. Going by Shinkansen[116] and Chūgoku
    Expressway
I parted from Tokyo and my blood relatives.
Around the graves, brown stick insects, green
Stick insects, blister beetles and mosquitoes swarm.
Greater cicadas swarm. Mother-in-law's
Plain-wood altar tablet was still on top of the gravestone
Where father-in-law placed it when the ashes were laid to rest.
    Father-in-law's
Movements were slow. Irritatingly
Slowly he washed the grave. The grave next door
Was for siblings who died last year and this year. The earth,
Heaped up in the shape of two coffins side by side,
Was sheltered by a wooden roof. The roof had weathered and
    changed colour,
The heap of earth was soft: beneath them the two
Six-year-olds were decomposing. Schoolchildren's
Yellow umbrellas had been planted in the soil. From the
    posthumous names
I tried to picture the real names of the two six-year-olds.
Father-in-law stamped on the stick insects and
Carried on washing the grave. Tokyo and my blood relatives,
    father-in-law and my husband
Think that it is me in this grave.

Bad breasts[117]

The hot wind blew
Plants grow wild
Insects breed
Hot and humid

Plants grow wild
Insects breed
In the tropical depression
Rain sprinkles a white whirlpool
Plants grow wild
Trussed up for removal
Me trussed up
Every part of me trussed up
Turns into
Breasts
Insects breed
Breasts swollen, not to be drunk dry in the morning
Because they are sucked incessantly
By nightfall they are shrivelled and nothing comes out.

Bad faith
Me.

Because they are sucked incessantly
They are shrivelled and nothing comes out of me
Bad faith
My enormous breasts.

From good breasts
To bad breasts
On bad breasts
Babies plot revenge.

It is raining so we want to eat breasts
Clouds are scudding so we want to eat breasts
Winds are raging so we want to eat breasts.

Rain sprinkles a whirlpool so we want to eat breasts
When the rain stops
We can gather tasty yams
We can gather tasty taros
We can gather tasty bulbils
Tasty bean jam
Tasty faggot worms

Tasty acorns
Tasty starch
We can gather more than two hands can carry.

When the rain stops we can gather tasty taros
More than two hands can carry.

Glenn Gould Goldberg

Photo of Gu Gu sitting in a chair
Gu Gu bending backwards photo
Gu Gu staring photo
Photo of Gu Gu squatting
Photo of the back of a reclining chair
Bending backwards photo
Staring photo
Photo of Gu Gu resting his chin on his hands
Photo of Gu Gu's cheeks, mouth, clean-shaven
Distorted
Staring photo
Photo of Gu Gu crouching
Staring photo
Photo of Gu Gu's dog
Photo of Gu Gu peeping
Photo of a finger staring
Zound of boice zinging[118]
Gu
Static
Foreign static
Photo of a chair staring
Gu Gu
Photo of a chair vending vackwards
Photo of vinger zdaring
Chair doing penance, no, doing benanze
Vodo of a vinger
Dense and zdaring

Notes

1. This courting-song, with its enumeration of place names, is not unlike the later *michiyuki*, 'lovers' journey' (see page 121 ff.). On his way to Kohata, the Emperor met a pretty girl, asked her name, and promised to call on her on his return the following day. He was invited into her house, feasted, and sang this song as she served him wine. From the crab set before him at the feast, there is a transition in line 5 to the Emperor's adventure with the girl.

The places mentioned are on the west coast of Lake Biwa.

p. 4. **2.** The topic of the poem is the Prince's illicit love for his sister.

p. 7. **3.** A woman 'tells her name' to signify her assent to a proposal of marriage.

4. Pillow-word to Yamato. A dragonfly touches its tail with its mouth, thus forming a shape not unlike the circle of hills that ring Yamato.

p. 8. **5.** A talisman against misfortune on a journey.

p. 10. **6.** See the third *tanka* by Princess Nukada, above.

7. Princess Kagami had lost Emperor Tenji's favour to her younger sister, Princess Nukada.

p. 13. **8.** There is a pun on the name, Shii, and *shii-gatari*, a far-fetched story.

9. Empress Jitō, during whose reign (687–96) the Fujiwara Palace was first occupied. The timbers were carried overland for the short distance between the Uji and Izumi Rivers.

p. 15. **10.** Isonokami Shrine (the 'Shrine above the Stone') is south of Nara, above Furu River and on the lower slopes of Furu Hill.

p. 16. **11.** A *sedōka* (see Introduction).

p. 17. **12.** Japanese commentators are agreed that this is a political poem, but are unable to pinpoint the allusions in 'turtle-dove' and 'wagtail'.

13. This poem borrows the Chinese tradition that a girl named Kōga stole the elixir and made off with it to the Moon.

p. 18. **14.** A congratulatory opening.

15. 'To the land of Kara . . . eightfold' is an elaborate *jo* (preface) to the name Heguri and its pillow-word, 'Sloping smooth as eightfold mats'. Kara is Korea.

p. 19.   **16.** A series of word-plays. *Asu*, tomorrow, and the place Asuka: *oku*, to put down, and the place Okina: *tsuku*, to plant a staff, and the place Tsukuno, Tsuku Plain.

p. 20.   **17.** Probably the Kiso Highway, begun in 702 and opened in 713.

p. 24.   **18.** In Yamato.

p. 26.   **19.** Stone (*Ishi*) River was probably the site of a cremation-ground.
          20. The smoke of cremation is often described as a cloud.

p. 27.   **21.** The Haya, a southern Kyūshū tribe famous for the clarity of their voices, were employed at the Imperial Palace as watchmen.
          22. See note 3.

p. 29.   **23.** An Emperor of the Wei Dynasty (third century AD) in China prohibited *sake*: as a result, drinkers secretly called pure *sake* 'sage' and rough *sake* 'worthy'.
          24. The Seven Sages of the Bamboo Grove in Chin Dynasty China (third century).

p. 30.   **25.** Chêng Ch'üan, a Chinese who loved his wine, once said, 'Bury me at the side of an oven and, after a few hundred years, I may turn into a *sake* jar.'
          26. Buddhism likened its doctrines to a priceless jewel.

p. 31.   **27.** Drinking was one of the five prohibitions of Buddhism.
          28. A paraphrase of a passage in *Dai Nehan-kyō*.

p. 32.   **29.** The headnote says, 'Munakatabe Tsumaro, who was appointed helmsman of a ship ferrying provisions to the island of Tsushima, asked Arao, a lifelong shipmate, to take his place. Arao went down with his ship in a storm, whereupon his wife and children composed these poems.' There is an early tradition attributing the poems to Okura, at the time Governor of Chikuzen Province.

p. 40.   **30.** The 'Eastland' – the present Chiba-Ibaraki area.

p. 41.   **31.** Ten miles east of Tokyo.
          32. Suminoe Shrine, later called Sumiyoshi Shrine (see note 49) gave protection to seafarers.

p. 45.   **33.** One of the Korean kingdoms, in the south-east of the peninsula.

p. 46.   **34.** In the Hiroshima area.

p. 50.   **35.** On Iki Island.

p. 55.   **36.** Greed and evil in this life led to an after-life as a 'famished devil', always hungry yet never able to get food. Images of such devils were displayed in Buddhist temples as a warning. To worship them was pointless.

p. 67.   **37.** Literally 'Fifth Street': one of the ten main east-west streets in Kyōto.

p. 70.   **38.** Ōsaka, literally 'Meeting Hill' or 'Meeting Barrier', was a barrier between Kyōto and Ōtsu at which customs were collected and troops stationed. Narihira would pass this way travelling from the capital to Ise. The allusions and associations in the word were too good for the Japanese poet to miss (see also page 99 and note 53).

p. 71.   **39.** A pun on the two meanings of *nagame*, 'long rain' and 'gaze at'.

p. 73.   **40.** It was thought that clouds blocked the fairies in the sky from walking their customary paths. The poem was written on seeing a court dance (*Gosetchi no Mai*) and was for the maidens who danced.

p. 75.   **41.** Written on the eve of his departure for exile in Kyūshū and addressed to the plum-tree in his garden.

p. 78.   **42.** The headnote says that the poem was composed on parting from a woman with whom he had conversed at the side of a spring in the Shiga Hills.

p. 79.   **43.** Wild geese migrate north with the early spring, thus showing a completely un-Japanese disregard for the cherry-blossom.

p. 80.   **44.** As a charm to make the one you love appear in your dreams.

p. 81.   **45.** In Iwashiro, five hundred miles east of Kyōto.
         46. South-west of Tokyo.

p. 83.   **47.** Isonokami Shrine (see page 15 and note 10) was famous for its precious sword.

p. 85.   **48.** The river Kamo flows north-south through the eastern part of Kyōto.

p. 86.   **49.** See note 32.

p. 87.   **50.** The villa of Taira Kiyomori, headquarters of the Taira clan and, for the year 1180, the capital. On the site of the present Kōbe, it was fifty miles south-west of Kyōto.

         51. A nunnery at the foot of Mount Hiei, north of Kyōto. The former Empress Kenrei-monin, daughter of Taira Kiyomori and consort of Emperor Takakura (reigned 1169–80), retired from the world and spent the rest of her life there after her son, infant-Emperor Antoku, had been drowned and the armies of the Taira clan defeated by the Minamoto clan at the battle of Dan-no-ura in 1185.

p. 89.   **52.** Buddhist goddess of mercy.

p. 99.   **53.** See note 38.

p. 101. **54.** A fishing village on the west coast of Lake Biwa, famous for the net techniques of its fishermen.

p. 102. **55.** *Kasa* means both 'umbrella' and 'the halo of the moon'.

p. 105. **56.** *Hana yori dango* – pudding rather than praise: a reference to indifference to cherry-blossoms on the part of the wild goose (see note 43).

57. Asked to compose a *haiku* which would incorporate the Eight Famous Views of Ōmi, Bashō skilfully fulfils the request. Apart from the Evening Bell at Mii Temple, the rest of the Eight are visual in appeal and include Evening Snow on Mount Hira and Flight of the Wild Geese at Katada. Mii Temple is near Ōtsu, at the southern tip of Lake Biwa.

p. 106. 58. Written at Takadate, the 'Castle on the Height', where Yoshitsune, a Minamoto general, and his faithful followers were killed by the armies of his jealous brother.

p. 113. 59. Green and white are thought to be a good colour match: the white of Fuji's snow and the pink of cherry blossom do not blend.

p. 116. 60. The context is a fight between a fat frog and a lean and skinny one.

61. At Nara.

p. 117. 62. His stepmother's.

63. The ducks that survived New Year feasting.

p. 118. 64. The allusions or the links of feeling or thought which establish the chain are often difficult to grasp. In outline they are: Early winter rain (1) linked to the wind (2) followed by stillness. The wild landscape in 3 leads to a wild, man-scaring animal (4). Bows to scare badgers are placed over a house-frame, with the moon peeping over (5): the house in 5 is still inhabited by its old, stingy owner (6) who delights in sketching (7). Transition from late autumn in 7 to winter in 8; winter peace and quiet (9), the requisite of the artist. Tranquillity (10) as in the hills, hills such as Mount Ōmine in Yamato where the mountain ascetics practise their rites: their austerities ended, they come down off the hills and blow their conch-shells when they first see a village. Travellers (11) eating lunch at a tea-house with frayed mats hear the conch-shell. Near the tea-house is a pond where the lotus grows (12); the lotus is a symbol of purity and the mountain ascetics also offer purification. The lotus is in bloom when old friends gather (13) in a temple to eat a meal starting with laver (a water plant), a product for which Suizenji, near Kumamoto in Kyūshū, is famous. As one of the guests has a long walk home (14), he leaves early. Rodō, a T'ang poet, wrote the classic on tea and his old servant (15) would offer tea to passers-by. In such a household, servants stay on over the years. The statement of spring begins a new theme, of tranquillity. The cutting (16) and Rodō's servant both take root. The work of the gardener links 16 and 17 and the subject of 18 is at peace (back to 15) once in his garden. The recluse gardener, living alone, avoids bother (19) by cooking and eating two days' rice at one time: on an island off the north coast, fishermen going out on a long expedition eat two days' food before they sail (20). At the hill temple of this island, a beacon is lit for passing ships (21). As he climbs the island hill, the lamplighter reflects that the cuckoos are silent in the dusk (22). The silence is the link with (23), the silence of the sick-room and the patient's alarm at the swift change of the seasons. In one episode in *Genji Monogatari*, Genji visits his old nurse who is sick and finds the gate locked; as he waits, he notices the house next door (24) which belongs to Lady Yugao, his future love. The sounds of a carriage (25) disturb a secret lovers' meeting. In 26, after a secret meeting, a *samurai* is handed his forgotten sword as he goes: the woman then straightens her hair (27), the link with 28, the loose woman doing up her hair after getting up from her bed. In spite of such disturbed emotions, the dawn is serene (29) as is early autumn on Lake Biwa, the water reflecting Mount Hira's shape (30). Buckwheat, grown on the slopes of Hira, is harvested in autumn (31), its small flowers looking like frost. With the cold autumn evenings, men go into padded clothing (32). At a cheap inn, with not enough bedclothes, guests sleep huddled together for warmth and then set out individually in the morning (33). Morning clouds over Mount Tatara in Kyūshū appear lonely (34). The Tatara area was famous for the leather work of its colony of Korean immigrants (35); workers in leather, outcasts, live a lonely life in contrast with the joy inspired by the cherry-blossom. There is joy and hope in new growth (36), living alongside the old and the decayed.

p. 121. **65.** The reference is to a tradition, originally Chinese, that the two stars, the Herdsman and the Weaving Girl, meet only once in the year, on the seventh night of the seventh month, crossing over a sky-bridge built by magpies from their feathers. The River of Heaven is the Milky Way.

p. 122. **66.** A popular ballad of the day.

p. 123. **67.** The places described on the journey, Tenjin Grove, Umeda Dyke and Sonezaki Grove are all in or on the outskirts of Ōsaka where the play is set.

68. Tokubei takes over the sentence in mid-construction, as often in Japanese drama.

69. A reference to the superstition, still prevalent, that certain ages were critical, among them twenty-five and forty-two for men, nineteen and thirty-three for women.

p. 124. 70. The deities of Shintō.

71. In certain Amidist sects, it was held that devout believers are reborn from a lotus after a period of five hundred years within it.

72. The red-light district in Edo.

p. 126. 73. The reference is to the mother-in-law.

74. The first cuckoo and first *bonito* of the season.

p. 127. 75. Not all want to go on to the red-light district.

p. 128. 76. In a *Nō* drama the deuteragonist often has long periods without any lines.

77. The flute in the *Nō* drama, often used to signify the link between movements or sections, bursts in with *forte* leads after long rests.

p. 129. 78. She cut it off as a vow when she was a prostitute.

79. The subject is a prostitute: the language is that of the Yoshiwara.

p. 131. 80. A reference to the great vogue of the *kyōka*. There is an allusion to a *haiku* of Bashō:

> First winter drizzle:
> The monkey, too, looks to need
> His own straw raincoat.

In the hills on the road to Ise, a monkey in the top of a tree looks forlorn in the rain blown by the cold wind of early winter.

81. In his Preface to *Kokinshū*, Tsurayuki had said: 'Poetry, without effort, can move heaven and earth.' (See page lxii.)

p. 133. 82. The Japanese see a hare, rather than a man, in the moon.

p. 134. 83. Past, present, and future.

p. 138. 84. A wrestling figure that never falls over.

p. 141. 85. A 'counting-song' (*kazoe-uta*) usually has the appropriate number at the head of each line, it being followed by a word beginning with the same *kana* syllable as the number word. Japanese number words are used most commonly, but here the Chinese numbers are used: thus, (five) *go*, with the following word beginning *goki* . . . ; (six) *roku*, followed by *roku*. . . . We have tried to preserve this feature by repeating the initial consonant or vowel sound of the number word.

p. 146. 86. Shinjō is the home town of the loved one.

p. 151. 87. The Twenty-Five Bodhisattvas of Amitābha's retinue.

p. 156. 88. A temple (literally 'Hall of the Poet Immortal') in the hills north of Kyōto.

89. This place-name is loaded: see pp. 40–1 and note 95.

p. 157. 90. The juice of the snake-gourd is used to stop the formation of phlegm.

p. 158. **91.** Open-air *Nō* is performed at shrines in Tokyo, Kyōto, etc.

92. Kyōto dialect has many soft and silky sounds.

p. 159. **93.** This *haiku* was composed in Kew Gardens in May 1936 and is now recorded in the original Japanese and in this English translation on memorial stones in the Japanese Garden near the restored Japanese Gate.

p. 160. **94.** The red cicada is the last to die.

p. 161. **95.** See note 89.

96. Silkworms, when awake, can be unexpectedly noisy.

p. 163. **97.** March, when wild geese migrate to the north (see note 43), is the time of final examinations, when undergraduates have no time for anything but last-minute revision.

p. 165. **98.** On the day of the Boys' Festival, 5 May, pennants in the shape of carp are flown at the head of a bamboo mast by houses in which there are sons. The carp, fighting its way up river, is regarded as a fitting model of persistence and valour.

p. 166. **99.** The pilgrimage to the Shrine of the Sun Goddess at Ise was often undertaken by local associations (particularly of old people) and provided a good excuse for a long gossip.

p. 175. **100.** Russian for 'To the People'.

p. 176. **101.** A three-stringed musical instrument which is plucked.

p. 182. **102.** A Tokyo ward.

p. 186. **103.** Satō refers to his love for Chiyo, the first wife of novelist Tanizaki Junichirō, whom he married in 1930.

p. 188. **104.** Internal sliding partition, of paper panes on a wood framework.

105. The *Taipings*, who rebelled in China in the mid nineteenth century, marked their faces.

p. 190. **106.** The battle for Saipan was one of the turning-points in the Pacific War. Imperial Headquarters had boasted that this shield behind which Japan sheltered was impregnable.

p. 191. **107.** Two of the masks worn by *Nō* actors; *Mikenjaku* has long eyebrows and lashes.

p. 192. **108.** A wide divided skirt of thick silk, worn by men on formal occasions.

p. 206. **109.** A knee-length cloak, usually black and patterned with family crests.

110. The main shopping street in Tokyo.

111. *Symbol of Anguish*, by Kuriyagawa Hakuson (1880–1923).

p. 211. **112.** All are popular tourist resorts.

p. 213. **113.** A large office block in Tokyo.

p. 227. 114. Mindanao, in the Philippines, was the scene of fierce fighting in the Pacific War.

p. 229. 115. She uses the jargon of the late 1950s.

p. 253. 116. Shinkansen is the high-speed rail network of Japan Rail.

117. Itō Hiromi borrows Melanie Klein's concept of 'good breasts and bad breasts'.

p. 255. 118. Itō Hiromi plays with words, coining new ones by substituting consonants and vowels (the *kana* syllabary) in regular patterns. (See Introduction, p. xlvii.)

Index of Poets